# AND DISTRICT

## VOLUME 2

BY

### Dr. Haldane Mitchell

A Rotary contribution to local history

*To Suzanne, Angus and Fergus*

Published by the Rotary Club of Omagh.

November 1991.

© Copyright reserved.

ISBN 0 9516810 1 X

Designed and printed by
Graham & Sons (Printers) Ltd., Omagh, Co. Tyrone.

*Front cover photograph:* High Street, 1906.
*Rear cover photograph:* Lovers' Retreat in Victorian times

# Foreword

by Dr. Haldane Mitchell

'President of the Rotary Club of Omagh (Chartered 1955)

*F*ollowing the publication of volume one, I received many letters from all over the world — it's amazing where Omagh people get to.

To all those who contacted me in any way I am most grateful.

The photographic camera is 150 years old and through its many lenses many images have been recorded.

In this volume I have tried to cover a great many of those years with Omagh people at work, at war, at peace, at play, and the many changes which have taken place through development and growth.

A vehicular theme runs through this volume as a tribute to the members of Omagh Motor Club, with whom I have been associated for many years.

*Haldane Mitchell.*

# Significant Dates in History of Omagh and Contemporary Ireland

## EARLY TIMES TO 1609

### OMAGH

**1397** John Colton, Archbishop of Armagh, passes through Cappagh on way to Ardstraw.

**1430** Approximate date of erection of the 'Old Castle' (Castle of Omagh) by Art O'Neill, son of Eoghan O'Neill, Prince of Ulster (1432-1455).

**1455** Art O'Neill (Art of Omagh) dies.

**1459** Henry O'Neill, brother of Art of Omagh, and Prince of Ulster (1455-1483), led a force of Anglo-Normans to Omagh Castle to wrest it from sons of Art O'Neill.

**1464** House of Franciscan Third Order Regular founded in vicinity of Abbey Street.

**1470-71** Henry O'Neill takes Castle of Omagh from sons of Art O'Neill — Niall Mac Airt and his brothers.

**1498** A Host of Irish and Foreigners (Gaedhil and Gaill) compel Nial MacAirt in Castle of Omagh to give hostages.

**1509** The Lord Deputy (Earl of Kildare) at the invitation of sons of Conn Mor O'Neill (1483-1493) — Art Og and Conn Bacach — marches against Castle of Omagh and razes it to the ground.

**1512** O'Donnell, Prince of Tyrconnell, restores 'in a week' the Castle which had been demolished by Earl of Kildare and leaves a garrison there.

**1514** Castle of Omagh again broken down by Art Og O'Neill, Prince of Ulster (1513-1519).

**1517** Chiericati, Papal Nuncio to England, describes 'Nomach', the district of Omagh.

**1538** Castle of Omagh again demolished by Niall O'Neill.

**1602** Lord Mountjoy, Lord Deputy, places garrison in Omagh under Sir Henry Dowcra.

**1603** Franciscan Friary and lands taken by Capt. Edmond Leigh.

**1609** District of Omagh (Barony of Omagh) granted to George Audley, later Lord Castlehaven, and family.

### IRELAND

**c.300 B.C.** Foundation of Eamhain Macha (Emania) or Armagh.

**331 A.D.** Foundation of Oirghialla (Oriel).

**379-405** Reign of Niall of the Nine Hostages.

**425** Aileach dynasty established.

**432** St. Patrick's Second Coming to Ireland.

**795** Invasion of Ireland by the Norsemen.

**1014** Battle of Clontarf.

**1148** Oirghialla and Ulaidh submit to Muircertagh MacLochlainn.

**1169** Coming of the Normans.

**1171-72** Henry II in Ireland.

**1210** King John comes to Ireland.

**1241** Battle of Caimeirghe. Brian O'Neill defeats MacLochlainns.

**1281** Hugh Buidhe O'Neill defeats Donal O'Donnell at Desertcreight.

**1315** Edward Bruce lands in Ireland.

**1394-95** Expedition of Richard II to Ireland.

**1423** Eoghan O'Neill defeats Lord Deputy Talbot.

**1430** Midland chiefs submit to Donal O'Neill, Prince of Ulster (1403-1432).

**1455-1485** Wars of the Roses in England.

**1477-1513** Garret Mor Fitzgerald, 8th Earl of Kildare.

**1487** Lambert Simnel crowned King in Christ Church, Dublin.

**1492** Columbus discovers America.

**1522** O'Donnell of Tirchonaill (Tyrconnell) defeats Conn Bacach O'Neill (1519-1559) at Knockavoe, near Strabane.

**1541** Henry VIII assumes title of King of Ireland.

**1542** Conn Bacach O'Neill created Earl of Tyrone.

**1567** Defeat and death of Shane O'Neill (1559-1567).

**1595** Hugh O'Neill becomes Earl of Tyrone.

**1601** Battle of Kinsale.

**1603** Submission of Hugh O'Neill at Mellifont.

**1607** Flight of the Earls.

**1608-1609** Plantation of Ulster.

Dr. John Wishart Winchester, M.D., B.Ch., D.M.R.E., F.F.R. (1901-1980) was the first President of the Rotary Club of Omagh in 1955.

'Jock', as he was affectionately known, was born in Scotland, the son of a school-teacher. He qualified in medicine at St. Andrew's in 1924.

He saw service in Borneo after which he took charge of the Chest Hospital in Singapore.

He spent much of the war as a prisoner of the Japanese, first in Changi and then as a Camp Medical Officer to the large civilian camp at Sime Road between 1943-1945.

In 1951 he joined the staff of Tyrone County Hospital as the first Consultant Radiologist. He continued in post until his 75th birthday when no replacement was available.

A true gentleman.

# Sweet Omey

## By David McClelland

Sweet Omey town with all around
Your sights of beauty rare,
Go where you may in Summertime,
With you none can compare.
Why should we spend our hard-earned gold
Some far-off land to see
When we have here Dame Nature's hand
Displayed so lavishly?

Although the broad Atlantic
Breaks not upon our shore,
Our inland scenes are beautiful,
We ask for nothing more.
The hand of man is here unseen —
All this the Almighty made,
And our fond memories linger round
The beauty here displayed.

Seek Lisanelly's wooded grounds,
And then look down and see
The silver Strule flow racing past
And dancing in its glee.
The giant oaks and beeches tall
Stand pointing to the sky,
A lovely place 'tis said to be
By every passer by.

There's Lisnamallard and Glencree
And lovely Riverdale,
A murmuring breeze springs through the trees
And whispers in the vale.
Cool winding walks and avenues,
Demesnes broad spread and fair,
Plantations on the western side
Skirt Omey, over there.

Glenhordial's lofty peak we reach
And view the landscape o'er,
A sight most grand, our view commands,
Far reaching to Dromore.
And woods of Rash. If I could sing
Old Omey! You'd see how I adore
Our friendly hills around her spires —
Once the Abbey of Gortmore.

Sweet Edenfel, no tongue can tell
The beauty you possess,
And Crevenagh's kindly, haunting bower
Her charms are nothing less;
The old Leap Bridge, its waterfall
With rippling music sweet;
And last we turn our steps toward
The Lovers' loved Retreat.

*Tyrone and Fermanagh Hospital.*
*This is one of Omagh's finest buildings and probably the largest. It was built in 1847-53 from a design by William Farrell at a cost of £35,000. In 1863 extensive additions were made by George Boyd. Catholic and Protestant chapels were built in 1901 and 1903.*

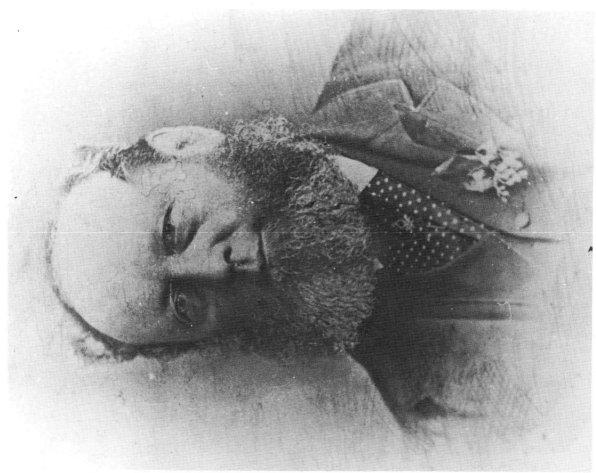

Dr. Francis John West, M.D., M.R.C.S.E., was the first Resident Medical Superintendent of the institution. The hospital opened for the reception of patients on 2nd May, 1853, and the complete minutes of all meetings of the Board of Governors and Guardians are to be found in a bound collection in the hospital, giving its history from its inception. Dr. F. J. West died in service on 23rd October, 1880. There is a memorial window to his life and work in St. Columba's Parish Church, Omagh.

*Tyrone and Fermanagh Hospital was originally called the Omagh District Asylum. Board of Governors circa 1895:*
*Standing: Edward Boyle, J.P., R. J. Creery (Clerk), Dr. McKelvey (A.M.O.), Hugh de F. Montgomery, D.L., James Brown, J.P., Miss McFarland (Matron), Dr. G. E. Carre (R.M.S.), Col. L. M. Buchanan, D.L.*
*Seated: W. C. Trimble, R. Harvey, J.P., M. Devlin, J.P., Rt. Rev. Mgr. McNamee, P.P., J. G. Crozier, J.P., Rt. Hon. Viscount Corry, D.L.*

*Tyrone and Fermanagh Mental Hospital — Senior Officers and Male Staff 1945.*
*Back row from left: J. Coyle, J. McManus, P. Kelly, A. Smith, J. Thompson, G. Boyle, J. Flanagan, W. Ross, J. Allen, S. Donaghy, C. Ross, R. Duncan.*
*Third row: P. Breen, J. McMichael, J. O'Donnell, P. McSwiggan, L. Porter, H. McSwiggan, A. McAleer, A. Greer, F. Scullion, M. McCormick, J. McLean, T. Ewing, G. Patterson, F. McQuade, J. Gilmour.*
*Second row: R. Ewing, T. Bell, B. Wilkinson, F. Lilley, J. Kyle, F. Coyle, C. Shannon, J. McCanny, P. Mullan, T. Coyle, T. Baker, W. Steele, W. Duncan, J. J. Maguire, H. Johnston, E. Moss, G. Maguire.*
*First row: Wm. Ballantine, J. Ingram, O. L. Walsh, David Barbour, Miss I. Guy, Dr. W. Kelly, Dr. M. Roche, Dr. J. Moore Johnston, Dr. J. E. Herbert, Miss Robb, Miss Marion Mitchell, J. McConkey, Mrs. M. McFarland, H. Ronaldson, F. Patterson.*

## Tyrone and Fermanagh Hospital — Senior Officers and Female Nursing Staff 1946.

*Back row from left: Miss Edith Elliott, Omagh, Clerical Staff (now Mrs. Anderson); Miss E. Gardiner, Fintona, Student Nurse (now Mrs. Graham); Miss Mabel McKinley, Killygordon, Donegal, Student Nurse (now Mrs. Wm. Lindsay, Portstewart); Miss Nora Leonard, Fermanagh, Student Nurse (now Mrs. Quigley, Omagh); Miss Agnes Coyle, Mullaslin, Student Nurse (now Mrs. Joe Flanagan, Omagh); Miss Bridget Devine, Sixmilecross, Student Nurse, Omagh; Miss Eliz. Grieve, Donemana, Student Nurse (now in Australia); Miss Daisy Cashel, Tempo, Student Nurse (now Mrs. Foster, Omagh); Miss C. O'Kane, Drumquin, Staff Nurse (now Mrs. McDonald, Omagh); Miss B. Meenagh, Mullaslin, Student Nurse (now Mrs. Owen Nugent, Carrickmore); Miss E. Barbour, Omagh, Staff Nurse; Miss A. McFarland, Omagh, Clerical Officer (D).*

*Middle row: Mr. William Kyle, Omagh, Assistant Chief Male Nurse (D); Miss K. B. McNulty, Dromore, Ward Sister (D); Miss M. C. Morris, Drumquin, Ward Sister (D); Miss Cassie McCreery, Donegal, Ward Sister (D); Miss Annie Gorman, Mountfield, Ward Sister (D); Miss Margaret Browne, Ederney, Ward Sister (D); Miss Ena Boyd, Omagh, Ward Sister (D); Miss Annie Monaghan, Lisbellaw, Ward Sister; Miss May Clarke, Sixmilecross, Depouty Ward Sister; Miss Eliz. McCanny, Sixmilecross, Deputy Ward Sister; Miss Eliz. McCormack, Omagh, Staff Nurse (D); Miss Rosaleen McBride, Plumbridge, Student Nurse; Miss Mary Hall, Drumquin, Ward Sister (now Mrs. F. McDonald, Drumquin); Mr. Harry Johnston, Omagh, Deputy Chief Male Nurse (D).*

*Front row: Mr. William Ballantine, 16 Campsie Avenue, Omagh, Maintenance Staff (D); Miss Marion Mitchell, 14 Belvedere Park, Omagh, Catering Staff; Mr. Joseph Ingram, 10 Campsie Road, Omagh, Storekeeper (D); Miss Bella Guy, Donegal, Assistant Matron (became Mrs. Tubman) (D); Mr. David Barbour, Land Steward; Dr. Wilfred Kelly, Belfast, Medical Staff; Dr. Marion Roche, Newtownstewart, Medical Staff; Dr. J. Moore Johnston, Resident Medical Superintendent (D); Dr. J. Herbert, Enniskillen, Assistant R.M.S. (D); Miss E. Robb, Fintona, Matron (later Mrs. King, Bushmills); Mr. O. Louis Walsh, Augher, Hospital Secretary (D); Mr. John McConkey, Chief Male Nurse (D); Mr. Ronaldson, Maintenance; Mrs. McFarland, Omagh, Assistant Secretary (D); Mr. Fred Patterson, Omagh, Assistant Storekeeper (D).*

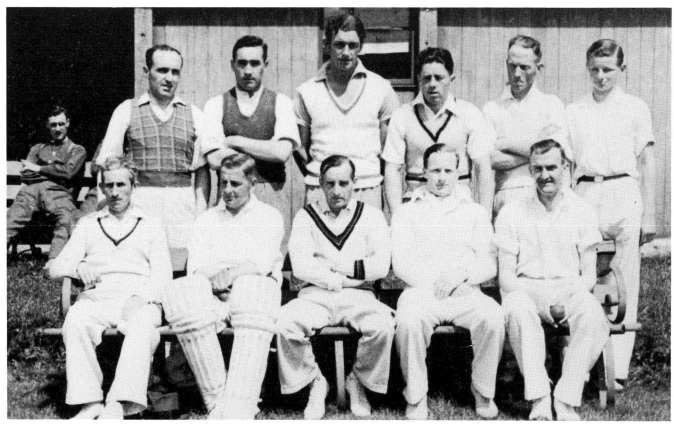

*Playing cricket at the Tyrone and Fermanagh Hospital was a very popular pastime especially in the 1940's and 1950's. The team had an advantage during the war years playing against resident army teams.*
*1941 — Back row: Wm. Duncan, Robert Duncan, Paddy Kelly, Harry Kerr, Frank Coyle, Jim Walsh.*
*Front row: Charlie Reilly, Louis Walsh, Dr. J. M. Johnston, Dr. Glancy, Hugh Coyle.*

*Tyrone and Fermanagh Hospital Cricket XI which won the Tyrone and Fermanagh Cup in 1950, beating Dungannon Royal School, R.U.C. and Taylor Woods, Enniskillen.*
*Back row: Joe Keenan, William Moore, Tony Kelly, Robert Barbour, William Duncan, Frank Coyle, Rotarian Norman Armstrong (Scorer).*
*Front row: Jerry King, Derek Towell, Patrick Kelly, Dr. J. Moore Johnston, Hugh Coyle, Robert Duncan, D. B. T. Scott.*

In 1941 the Green Howards were stationed in Omagh. In their numbers were two England Test cricketers: Hedley Verity and Norman Yardley seen here in their cricketing whites with Dr. Moore Johnston (in blazer). Norman Yardley (centre) was an England Test selector after his Test career as a player ended. In 1941 a North-West XI played the Green Howards. The match, with photographs supplied by Jim Walsh, is mentioned in Alan Hill's "Hedley Verity — A Portrait of a Cricketer — 1986".

*Dr. Edward C. Thompson, D.L., M.B., F.R.C.S.I., resident surgeon at Tyrone County Hospital (1874-1928), seen here with his daughter Emy outside the surgeon's residence (Camowen Hill House) in his 1903 Turrel Light Car, made by Pollock Engineering Co. in Belfast. It had 2 cylinders and delivered 7 h.p. The roof of the Tyrone County Hospital is seen in the background.*

*J. R. G. Porter's horse-drawn hearse at Dublin Road Cemetery c.1910. The horseman is John Crawford. The men in uniform and the fact that the coffin is covered with the Union Flag suggests a military funeral.*

*Aerial view of High Street — probably the first ever taken by the Royal Flying Corps stationed at Strathroy Airfield during the First World War. The serial number is at the top right-hand corner and is dated 24/8/1918. Note the Picture House (Miller's) behind the Royal Arms Hotel, and the large repository behind Crawford and Wilson's shop which was built in 1916.*

*These two photographs taken in 1918 show the type of double-winged aircraft DH6's which flew from the grass airfield at Strathroy during the First World War. In this case a Lieut. Dick had a narrow escape when he crash landed his aircraft. The airman's uniform has changed very little over the years as seen in the second photograph.*

*Royal Inniskilling Fusiliers — group of past and present officers after Trooping the Colour on the King's Birthday, 1927. Many of these men saw service in Omagh.*

*Back row: Smith, Dooley, Moody, Rayner-Smith, Moody, Major Reilly, Brabazon, Cooper, Moore, Mahon, Braddell, Boyle.*

*Middle row: Atkins, Groombridge, Davidson, Williams, Stewart, Cotter, Butler, Nugent, Noble, Crossle, Hayes, Heard.*

*Front row: Verschoyle, Cockburn-Mercer, Noble, Major Hammond-Smith, Gen. Mackenzie, Lt.-Col. Smythe, Gen. Sir T. Clarke, Major Rothwell, Col. Stewart, Major Hewitt, Col. Reynolds, Major Cox, Major Willock.*

19

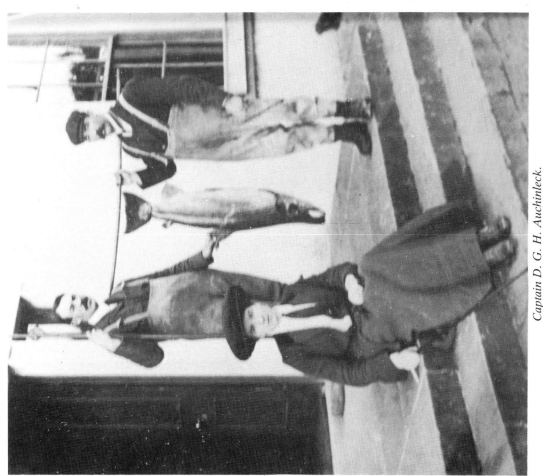

Captain D. G. H. Auchinleck.

Although born in Geneva, Switzerland, Daniel George Harold Auchinleck had his roots in Omagh at Crevenagh House. He was a keen fisherman. The photograph shows him and his gillie William Worling at his home at Laputa, Ballyshannon, after landing a 35 lb. salmon. The fish is still in the family's possession. His wife Madie is sitting on the step. Dan was also a keen golf and tennis player and played a part in forming both the Omagh and Bundoran Golf Clubs as well as the Omagh Lawn Tennis Club in 1892. Dan fought in the Boer War in 1899 with the 2nd Battalion Royal Inniskilling Fusiliers. He was also serving with the same regiment in Belgium during the First World War when he was killed on 21st October, 1914. He is buried in the Strand Military Cemetery, Ploegsteert, Belgium, a village 3 miles north of Armentieres.

Instructions regarding War Diaries and Intelligence
Summaries are contained in F. S. Regs., Part II.
and the Staff Manual respectively. Title pages
will be prepared in manuscript.

| Hour, Date, Place | Summary of Events and Information | Remarks and References to Appendices |
|---|---|---|
| 13th Oct. (continued) 14th " METEREN | in the neighbourhood of METEREN. fierce fighting, village taken during the night. Casualties Lieut D.H.P. Hartigan wounded 1 man killed + 8 wounded. Morning passed uneventfully. Considerable numbers of dead & wounded dealt with. Buried 14 Germans. Considerable amount of firing heard to the South. Batt. moved at 5 p.m. arrived at BAILLEUL at 9 p.m. Billetted. | Heavy rain during afternoon. |
| 15th " BAILLEUL | Received orders to move at 6 p.m. Halted for the night at 8 p.m. Bivouacked. | |
| 16th " PLOEGSTEERT | Ordered to march about 9 a.m. to PLOEGSTEERT with all precaution. Found town occupied by a cavalry brigade, and part of another pushed out on outpost line entrenched facing East. A certain amount of skirmishing by the cavalry patrols during the afternoon which died away towards nightfall. The enemy's patrols were located along the river. | |
| 17th " PLOEGSTEERT | Heavy artillery fire N. East of our position from 2 a.m. to 3.30 p.m. Received orders to move forward to LE GHEER and took up position on a line just east of village facing PONTROUGE, + passed a quiet night. | |
| 18th " LE GHEER | Cavalry pushed forward supported by Batt. to make a demonstration against PONTROUGE. The village was very heavily shelled + the cavalry brigade suffered very severely. In the evening the Batt. was ordered to HOUPLINES. | |
| 19th " HOUPLINES 20th " LE GHEER | Arrived at HOUPLINES at 5 a.m. Billetted. Ordered to return to LE GHEER. Enemy attacked our position at 9 a.m. & continued to press home the attack till 6 p.m. Our advanced posts were driven in. Casualties 6 men killed + 8 wounded. | |
| 21st " — do — | General attack on our trenches was successful. We were driven back a few hundred yards where we held the enemy from 5.15 a.m. till 10.30 p.m. at which time we reoccupied our forward trenches. Returned to billets in PLOEGSTEERT at 10 p.m. Casualties Capt. D.G.H. Auchinleck, Capt. S.G. Roe, + 2nd Lieut M. Roberts killed, 2nd Lieut F.J. Williams + 2nd Lieut A.C. Lyons wounded. 33 men killed, + 78 wounded. + 41 missing. | |
| 22nd " PLOEGSTEERT 23rd " ARMENTIERES 24th " | Billetted in PLOEGSTEERT. Ordered to ARMENTIERES. At ARMENTIERES. | |

*Extract from the War Diary showing date and place where Dan Auchinleck was killed. He is remembered by an inscription on a marble window ledge in the porch of Edenderry Parish Church with the words — "To the greater Glory of God, and the brave and gallant memory of Daniel George Harold Auchinleck, 2nd Battalion, Royal Inniskilling Fusiliers of Crevenagh, who fell in action near Le Gheer, Belgium, at dawn on 21st October, 1914". The Bell in the Church was given by Madeline his wife — with love and pride — Christmas 1918. She lived on at Crevenagh House until her death in 1949.*

# Omagh Barracks (now St. Lucia)

## *Extracts from the "Tyrone Constitution" of 1881.*

First reference found: Tyrone Constitution of —
(1) Friday, 2nd September, 1881.

### SOLDIERS FOR NEW BARRACKS

A fatigue party of 20 men from Enniskillen arrived in Omagh on Wednesday and pre-ceded by the local Militia Brass Band, which met them, marched to the new Barracks where they took up residence.

(This was probably the opening of Omagh Barracks, now St. Lucia — no pre mention is found but literature published in 1957 by the paper gave the opening date as September 31st (?), 1881 — no reference found in newspapers of this date, but mentioned the facts as above (2/9/81) as happening at opening of Barracks.)'

(2) Tyrone Constitution, 30th September, 1881.
Amusing fact mentioned: Omagh Cricket Club — vs — Royal Inniskilling Fusiliers: Omagh C.C. 45 All Out.    Royal Inniskilling Fusiliers — **27**.    Winners: Omagh.
(The regiment **did** score the correct number of runs at least.)

(3) Tyrone Constitution, 28th October, 1881.
Col. George Barst Stokes, who has been in Omagh since the arrival of the depot, is about to proceed to Preston. Thirty men of his regiment are expected to arrive in Omagh and take up quarters at the new Barracks.
(Could Col. Stokes have been first depot C.O.? Most interesting find as under, possibly written by a reporter on visit after opening of new Barracks.)

(4) Tyrone Constitution, Friday, 16th December, 1881.

### NEW MILITARY BARRACKS AT OMAGH

Some years ago the government purchased a piece of ground at the rear of the old Militia Barracks, Omagh, and on this have been erected buildings to meet all the requirements of a Brigade Depot Barracks which are now occupied by the 64th Brigade Depot, the old Militia Barracks being appropriated for the accommodation of the married staff.

On entering the front gateway of the new barracks we pass on the right the guard-house, a one-storey building with a verandah and flank towards the parade. Besides the prisoners' room, cells etc. this building also contains the Commanding Officer's office and Orderly room which are entered off the flank or parade front. Directly across the parade stands a large three-storey building, upwards of 300 feet long, the basement storey of which is utilised as stores and workshops, the two upper storeys being the men's barracks and accommodating 164 non-commissioned officers and men.

There are eight large barrack rooms in the building, and to each attached a spacious lavatory, etc., also a separate room for the non-commissioned officers in charge, with a small inspection window looking into the room. This block and the guard-house were built about three years ago, Messrs. Fulton Co. of Belfast being the contractors. They however remained unoccupied until recently.

At the rear of the soldiers' block just noticed stands the cook-house, a neat building, fitted up with Captain Warren's Army cooking apparatus.

Returning again to the Parade — which may here be observed is almost square and surrounded by the buildings — it had to be formed to suitable levels and gradients by excavating and removing some 30,000 tons of earth, and with the road which passes round it, has been coated with some 4,000 tons of stones and gravel.

On the west stands the officers' Mess and quarters — a very handsome building. Besides the Mess and Ante-rooms, and the usual appurtenances of an Officers' Mess, there are quarters in it for eight officers with accommodation for their servants in the basement storey. The field officers' quarters are connected with this building, but have separate entrances.

The internal fittings generally are most elegant.

The passages are laid with ornamental encaustic tiling, on a floor of concrete. It may be here noted that this kind of floor, finished smooth without tiles, obtains very much throughout, as all the passages, landings, corridors, kitchen, sculleries, yards, etc., have been laid of it. The ground floor windows are fitted with patent revolving shutters.

Polished mahogany presses, finely wrought Portland stone chimney pieces, etc., are found in all the officers' rooms and massive marble chimney pieces in the Mess and Ante rooms. All the other fittings are quite in keeping with the general character of the building.

In the North angle of the Parade is situated the officers' harness room and forage store. The stable fittings are all on the most approved modern principle.

On the East of the Parade, facing the officers' mess are erected the hospital and canteen, both large and elegant blocks. The hospital contains three wards with beds for 26 patients, a surgery waiting quarters for the hospital — sergeant, kitchen, etc.

At the rear are two isolated buildings — one the infectious ward, containing two beds, with an orderly's room attached, the other being the mortuary.

The canteen is a very commodious building, on the ground floor it contains the shop and tap with separate entrances, off the tap is a large tap room.

On the upper floor are the Recreation room, with coffee bar attached, and the reading room, both of which are reached by a separate entrance from the parade. On this floor also are quarters for the canteen-Sgt. and librarian.

By another door further on the right we enter the Sgts. Mess. The Mess room is large and commodious, a passage at the end of the room leads to the kitchen, cooks quarters, larder, store, scullery, etc. An extensive drill-shed has been erected, also a laundry and infants school, in the old barracks enclosure.

The buildings generally present a very handsome appearance, being built of the local limestone, with Dungannon grit-stone dressings. All the external walls are brick lined as a preventative to damp.

The town water supply has been laid on throughout the barracks with hydrants at convenient intervals in case of fire, and the entire barracks has been surrounded by a very substantial boundary wall with flanking chambers etc. built of the local stone, and coped with heavy concrete coping, standing eleven feet over surface of parade inside and varying from 12 to 20 feet outside. The wall is about 1800 feet long.

The works which cost from £30,000-£40,000 have been carried out in a most satisfactory manner by the Messrs. Colhoun Brothers of Derry, the superintending officer of the Royal Engineer Department being Mr. James H. Butler, C.E.

*Colours of 2nd, 9th, 13th and 4th Battalions of Royal Inniskilling Fusiliers at Officers' Mess, Omagh Barracks (St. Lucia), June 23rd, 1919.*

The Acade

Back row: —, Ted Duncan, —, Jim Adams, J. Neilands, W. McFarland, Stanley Moffitt, Sybil Pollock, —, — Foster, Edna Love, Muriel Love, Beatrice Alcorn,
Middle row: Maureen McMullan, Pearl Fullerton, A. Topping, Mattie Faux, Lil Wilson, M. Kerr, Myra Crammond, B. Harper, L. Thompson, D. Allison, Rebecca
Front row: David Mitchell, Dorothy Moorehead, V. Creery, Denise White, Helen Orr, —, Stanley Baker, Laura Creery, I. Pollock, A. Du

nagh, 1927

dwell, E. Anderson, —, David Adams, Fergus Gilmour, M. Kerr, Alex McKimmon, Harold Gwynne, Bobby Mitchell, Jack Wilson, —, Billy Blair, Bertie Parke.
McMullan, Mrs. Perdue, Mr. Perdue, Miss Burrows, —, — Johnston, Miss Osborne, I. Empey, R. Leitch, Phyllis Mitchell, Mollie Johnston, B. Lyttle, — Black.
Duncan, Monica Orr, Kitty Meadows, Mollie Duncan, Rosalie Orr, —, —, Jim McNeil, Bobby Maxwell, T. McCrea, — Meadows, — Baker.

25

# Omagh Academy — a short history

Like all other Irish country towns, Omagh has had a long tradition of educational achievement. The earliest available archive records of schools in the town date from the "Appendix to the Second Report from the Commissioners of Irish Education Inquiry" in 1826. At that time there were seven schools in the town, and although the numbers were disputed by the rival religious communities, the largest school recorded approximately 100 pupils on its roll and was maintained in a "neat slated house" costing £40 partly funded by the "Association for discountenancing vice".

Throughout the 19th Century interest in education grew as the town's population rose, and better communications brought the heart of Tyrone into wider contact with the outside world.

In the years between 1844 and 1859 announcements in the columns of the "Tyrone Constitution" indicate that a number of small private schools existed and were mostly conducted in the homes of teachers. One of these schools described as the "Abbey Hall Classical School" was under the Principalship of a Mr. Coen, a graduate of Trinity, who later returned to Dublin.

The provision of state assisted elementary education resulted in the opening of the Omagh Model School on 16th November, 1859.

In the following years several other schools opened their doors for the education of the small but growing middle class of the district who were able to afford boarding and other fees, and who wished their offspring to attain higher standards of education in the classics and so forth, than available at the Model School.

In the "Omagh Almanac and Co. Tyrone Directory" several of these establishments are recorded. As early as 1883, an "Intermediate School" operated at 3 Castle Street, run by the Rev. Samuel Paul (possibly Minister of Gillygooley Presbyterian Church). This school closed in 1903 after the Academy was founded.

There were also several private schools for girls in those days. "The Misses Adams Ladies' Boarding School" at 1 Campsie Road is recorded in the "Almanac" of 1885; and after 1887, this establishment moved to Market Street, becoming "The Ladies' High School, Omagh". It did not close until about 1920, when the girls from the school then began to attend the Academy. From an advertisement in the "Belfast Newsletter" of August 25th, 1903, the Ladies' High School boasted of a "Fully equipped Physical and Chemical Laboratory" with "good Music and Painting".

In 1886 a "Ladies' Select Boarding and Day School" under the Principalship of a Mrs. Douglas was opened at 12 Campsie Road, while in 1886 Monsieur and Madame Gambier ran the "Omagh Ladies' School" at 1 Campsie Road.

## FOUNDATION OF ACADEMY

After the beginning of the present century a group of prominent local people decided that it was time that Omagh had a Boys' Grammar School like many other towns throughout the country. As a result, a new independent school under a Board of Governors was established in March, 1903. From the "Rules for the Guidance of the Board of Governors", Rule 1 stated that, "The Name of the School shall be the Omagh Academy" and Rule 2 "The object of the Academy shall be the teaching of English, Mathematics, and Ancient and Modern Languages; and the promotion and encouragement of Intermediate Education for boys in all its branches".

The Board was to consist of 15 members with 5 ex-officio, viz: Two clergymen of the Church of Ireland; one the rector of Drumragh Parish Church, and the other to be nominated by him; Two Presbyterian clergymen, one the Minister in charge of First Omagh and the other in charge of Second Omagh Presbyterian Church; and the Methodist Clergyman on the Omagh Circuit or his deputy. The remaining ten were to be chosen by the vote of the Electors. The Electors were those parents paying fees or those persons subscribing a minimum of £1 per annum to the school.

The Board was to be first elected in October, 1906 and triennially thereafter, and was to be responsible for the affairs of the school. According to Rule 23 "The colours of the Academy shall be Navy Blue and Gold, and each pupil shall be required to wear a uniform Cap of Navy Blue, with the monogram 'O.A.' in gold," and Rule 25, "The work of the Academy shall be begun each day with reading of Scripture and prayer".

The first Board of Governors consisted of the following persons: Patron: His Grace the Duke of Abercorn; Chairman: Hans B. Fleming, M.B.; Hon. Secretary: William Cathcart, Strathroy, Omagh; Hon. Treasurers: Joseph Anderson, Market Street, Omagh; Thomas Johnston, Rosemount, Omagh; Committee: Rev. Canon Hayes, B.D., Rev. William A. Hayes, M.A., Rev. Andrew Macafee, B.A., David A. Clements, J.P., Percy G. Dallinger, M.A., Thomas C. Dickie, M.A., S.C.S., John Gray, W. Edmund Orr.

The new venture was welcomed in the local press:

"It must be extremely gratifying to those in charge of the project that the Omagh Academy is now an accomplished fact. When the matter was mooted we gave it our unqualified support and we therefore are glad to know that it has met with very general approval through the district. We do not for a moment insinuate that the other schools in the town are not admirable centres of learning in their way, but for several reasons into which we need not here enter, the Omagh Academy will supply a long-felt want in the district. As stated in the advertisement the school has been established to provide an intermediate education for boys in Omagh and neighbourhood. It affords all the advantages of a thorough and sound education in English, mathematics, experimental science, classics, foreign languages, and music, and will prepare boys for all grades of the intermediate, and for entrance to the Civil Service and matriculation to Universities. Two scholarships, to the value of £4 each will be awarded in June next year. The school is at present being conducted in the Y.M.C.A. rooms, but it is to be hoped that in the near future the governors will be in a position to have a properly equipped and up-to-date building of their own. The Headmaster is Mr. Henry A. Perdue, M.A., T.C.D., and the classical master, the Rev. J. A. Clarke". "The Tyrone Constitution", April 17th, 1903.

Shortly afterwards, the school moved to more permanent quarters in Market Street, on the site now occupied by Wellworth's Store. This three-storeyed building was formerly "The Abercorn Arms Hotel" owned by the Harkin family, and with its porch and stone steps which protruded into the street for some 8 or 9 feet, mahogany doors and stucco ceilings was originally "one of the best houses in the town". Behind it had a large garden with trees and shrubs stretching to the Dublin Road where a garage now stands. It was at this hotel that the famous "Liberator", Daniel O'Connell stayed, when he visited Omagh to speak in favour of Roman Catholic Emancipation. At one time the home of Mr. John Spiller, it later became the Post Office and continued as such until 1904, when it became the Academy. The School continued on this site until 1938, when the building was demolished to make room for the County Cinema.

The Academy quickly became established and by June 1903 has published its first examination results in the press and held a Sports Day. The school soon won many successes in the Intermediate Examinations but was always handicapped by lack of capital and by the old and unsuitable building in which it was housed.

Mr. Perdue resigned in 1935 and the school was transferred by the Governors to the Omagh Regional Education Committee, who appointed Mr. A. de G. Gaudin, M.A., as the new Headmaster. He resigned in 1937 on his appointment as Headmaster of Dungannon Royal School. During Mr. Gaudin's time the plans for new school buildings were finally approved. The number of pupils in attendance was then about 100 and it was decided that accommodation for about 180 would be more than sufficient.

For several years the Omagh Regional Education Committee sought a suitable site and at last the present site of the school was chosen. A new Headmaster, Mr. R. A. Simpson, B.A. (QUB), M.A. (Cantab.) was appointed in April, 1937, and the foundation stone of the new buildings was laid a few weeks later by Mr. Thomas Johnston, J.P., Chairman of the Omagh Regional Education Committee.

### NEW BUILDINGS OPENED

Just over a year later on Wednesday, 1st June, 1938, the new school buildings were officially opened by the Duchess of Abercorn, wife of the Governor of Northern Ireland, accompanied by the Minister of Education, Senator J. H. Robb, K.C., at a ceremony attended by many prominent local citizens.

The Vicereine was met at the school gates by Mr. Johnston, Chairman of the Educational Committee, and they proceeded to the main entrance of the building past lines of pupils from the Academy and the Technical School. As they approached the door, the Union Jack on the masthead was broken by Renee Alcorn and Edmund Giboney, senior pupils at the Academy. Mr. Johnston introduced the Vicereine to the Minister of Education, Senator Robb, members of the Regional Education Committee, members of Academy and Technical Committees, the Architects, and the contractor. Then, the Vicereine declared the buildings officially opened, and Senator Robb unveiled a bronze tablet on the corridor facing the main entrance door, commemorating the opening of the new buildings. The party proceeded to tour the school and then entered the Assembly Hall, now the Dining Hall, where speeches were made, congratulating the Education Committee and all others involved in this tremendous achievement.

The Education Minister said that this was one of the finest school buildings to be built in Ulster and that the new schools provided suitable accommodation for teaching, the British tradition of education. It was an education that was to fit men and women to think and act for themselves.

In reply to the Minister, Mr. Johnston thanked the Government of Northern Ireland for all their help and assistance to the building scheme, and for all that they were doing for the people of the Omagh area. The proceedings ended with afternoon tea in the Assembly Hall.

The headlines in "The Tyrone Constitution" announced "Accommodation Solved for Next Half Century". The building accommodated the Omagh Academy, the Technical School and the Administrative Buildings of the Omagh Regional Education Committee. The scheme cost £30,000 and a description of the schools was given in "The Tyrone Constitution" — Friday, 3rd June, 1938.

*Mr. and Mrs. H. A. Perdue with two members of staff and some pupils of the Academy in 1913. The boy standing in front of Mrs. Perdue is the late Dr. James McCauley of Ashdene, Campsie.*

28

*Garden party at the Academy in 1926 when these pupils performed "Cinderella".*
*Back row from left: Winnie Corker, married a man called Edelstein, father of Dr. George Edelstein (D) who pioneered chemotherapy at Belvoir Park Hospital, Belfast; Fred Corker, her brother, became a minister in America. (The Corkers were the family of the then Town Clerk); Phyllis Anderson, daughter of the owner of J. B. Anderson's; Emily Bradley (Campsie Avenue), daughter of Sergeant in R.U.C.*
*Front row from left: Ethel Wallace, daughter of Postmaster; William Empey, qualified as Medical Doctor; Rosalie Orr, daughter of Edmund Orr (The Grange), now Mrs. McClintock, Newtownstewart; Daphne Wright and Kathleen Wright, daughters of Northern Bank Manager; May Leitch, daughter of Solicitor who lived in Holmlea; Elsie Stewart (née Faux), 35 Dublin Road, Omagh.*

*The Academy — Regional Education Offices — Technical School, 1st June, 1938.*
*Pupils of both schools form a guard of honour waiting for the Duchess of Abercorn to arrive to perform the official opening.*

The official opening of the present Academy on 1st June, 1938, by the Duchess of Abercorn. This year, 1991, a multi-million pound extension will be opened officially. From left: Rev. J. H. R. Gibson, M.A. (Chairman, Omagh Technical College Instruction Comittee), Rt. Hon. J. H. Robb, K.C. (Minister of Education for N.I.), James Laffin (Builder), Robert Ferguson (Architect), P. J. Brennan (Headmaster of Technical College), Thomas Johnston, J.P. (Chairman of Education Committee and Board of Governors), Harold McCauley.

Miss Anne Brennan, daughter of the Headmaster, presents the bouquet to the Duchess.

*Omagh Academy only played hockey up until the end of the 1939-45 War when rugby became the main sport for the boys. Omagh C.B.S. had been playing rugby since the 1920s. North-West Ulster Schools Hockey XI played Leinster Schools in March, 1942, at Campsie Road and the team included five Academy players.*

*From left: Jim Walsh (Dept. of Agriculture, Zimbabwe), Victor Clarke (now retired bank manager), Arthur Jones (qualified M.B. etc. at Queen's — now a consultant psychiatrist), Howard Cathcart (lives near Beragh), Wray Watson (general medical practitioner and farmer near Raphoe, Co. Donegal).*

*Pupils from the Ladies' High School in Market Street going in two wagonettes for their annual outing in 1905. The site of the High School is occupied by the Northern Bank today and the Y.M.C.A. by the Tourist Information Centre. The site was originally the Tyrone Infirmary up until 1899. The rollers and ploughs outside the Y.M.C.A. are the property of Frank Crawford of Crawford & Wilsons. The firm continued to display their farm implements on this site until it was knocked down. Note McMillin's shop which was in business until some ten years ago when Rotarian Ronnie Hendly changed it to confectionery.*

*George F. Wilson's Drapery and Shoe Shop in High Street in 1905. Note the boots and shoes handing from a long piece of timber at the doorway and the holiday notice for a July holiday similar to the notices used by the Omagh District Council to the present day. George Wilson is standing in the doorway on the left while the man on the right is Alfred Clarke, an uncle of Stanley White (Derry Road). A. A. Love, father of Elsie Mullan, Ira and Edna Love (Breezemount Park), served his time in this shop at the turn of the century before setting up his own business in Market Street.*

*The Royal Arms Hotel in 1905 with staff of the Reform Stores standing on the pavement. The horse-drawn vehicle was the hotel bus to convey patrons to and from their destinations, mainly the railway station. The Hotel was built in 1787 and owned by the Porter family. It was occupied by the Americans in 1944 and they flew the Stars and Stripes from the flagpole. It has been under the management of the Waterson family since 1959. The Rotary Club meets in the Function Room each Thursday at 1 p.m.*

*Omagh's first 'Leisure Centre' was at Lough Muck. About 1930, this elaborate swimming complex was built half-way down the east side of the lough. It included changing rooms and a long walkway out to the diving boards. There was also a water slide which could be kept moist using a stirrup pump. Some 50 yards from the diving boards was an anchored raft for the safety of swimmers. Ernie Scarffe supplied the timber to build the complex, while its building was carried out by Tom Bonar, Joe Potts, Tommy Redpath and others.*

*Lough Muck Amateur Swimming and Life-Saving Club, 1931.*
*Open day — a group of swimmers about to take the plunge. Note the variety of swimming trunks worn in the 1930's.*

*Loughmuck Amateur Swimming Club 1933.*
Back row: (seated) Mrs. Johnston, Alan Alcorn, Patsy McGrath, Mattie Faux, Bob McFadden, Curate Lee, Harry Maginnis, Canon Cullimore, (seated) Mrs. Moorehead, John McConnell.
Middle row: Rotarian Robin Waterson, Officer from Military Depot, Miss McGrath, Maureen McMullan, Jean Faux, Miss McGrath, Robert Black.
Front row: Robert Waterson (Club President and Captain), Thomas Redpath, Joe Potts, Nelson Rountree (Past District Governor, Rotary Ireland), Liam McGrath, George Maginnis, Thomas Bonar, William Dunbar, Drew Quinn.

*Tom Bonar in bathing suit pointing out life-saving details on a chart on the gent's bathing box. Tom was a sergeant in the R.U.C. His favourite 'party piece' was to swim the length of Lough Muck in his full R.U.C. uniform, without hat of course, but with his boots on. His 'Houdini' act was to swim with his ankles tied and his hands tied behind his back.*

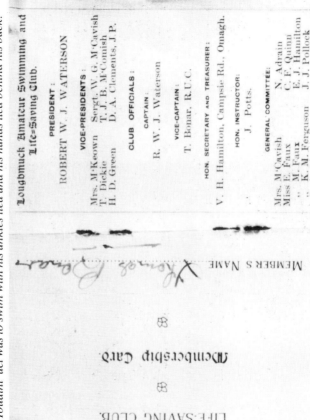

*Tom Bonar's membership card of the Lough Muck Amateur Swimming and Life-Saving Club. Life-saving was taught to all members and they were examined by visiting examiners from Belfast.*

# The Bard of Newtownstewart

## CORNABRACKEN SCHOOL

*Robert Kerr 23/11/1891-31/5/1916. Through his many poems about Newtown-stewart he will be remembered. 75 years ago this year he paid the Supreme Sacrifice in the Battle of Jutland when serving on H.M.S. Defence. He was the brother of Catherine Sloane who from the 1940's to 1970's owned Isaac Boyd's confectioner's shop in Lower Market Street. His poems were mainly written on active service and sent to the Tyrone Constitution where they were published under the pen-name of 'Arkey'.*

In a quiet country spot, on the landscape just
   a dot.
  Stands a house which all of late has gained
    some fame;
In the years that have gone past it has weathered
   many a blast,
  But never had such talk about its name.
As a seat of learning once there no doubt was
   many a dunce,
  Who never could keep his mind fixed on a
    rule,
But if what we hear is right, the present pupils
   are all bright,
  In the spooning class at Cornabracken school.

When the evenings aren't fine, for the school
   they make a line,
  And two by two they enter — not the ark.
Then commence their studies there, mighty
   queer you will declare,
  Yes, for all the teaching done is in the dark.
If at geometry he'd linger, the circumference of
   her finger,
  He'll be taught to find with cord and not by
    rule,
And for working out the date of the wedding
   there's no slate,
  In the spooning class at Cornabracken school.

The language that is spoken, may be English,
   but it's broken
  Into duckey, ookey, snookey, pussums, dear.
And it's marvellous how some of the staidest
   men become
  Loving fools when the departing time is near.
While outside the storm is raging, in the shelter
   they're engaging
  As the raindrips round their feet construct
    a pool,
But for wet feet they're not caring, as young
   cupid does the snaring
  In the spooning class at Cornabracken school.

If 'Inquisitive' has money, and can murmur
   words of honey,
  He'll be taken as a pupil right away,
And the terms he can bring; they are just a plain
   gold ring,
  And a visit to the parson, one fine day.
But some have cursed the fate that they were
   seen there of late;
  Now they vow to "shoot on sight that
    meddling fool",
So if you go there don't get seen, take the tip of
   one who's been
  In the spooning class at Cornabracken school.

*Soccer team on H.M.S. Defence 1912-1913 showing Robert Kerr first from the left on the back row.*

*The Loreto Convent — The Parlour or Music Room c. 1900.*

*Loreto Convent — Form 2A 1956-57*

Back row: Camilla Loughran, Alice Harpur, Geraldine McGinn, Rosaleen McQuade, Monica McGale, Dolores McGurk, Mary McQuade, Finnola McCrory, Susan Masters.
Middle row: Brona Donnellan, Mana Keys, Eliz. Anne McNally, Maura Hamill, Maureen McDonnell, Theresa Martin, Kathleen Currid, Nuala Higgins, Kathleen Muldoon, Eileen Conway, Rosaleen ——, Rosemary Donnelly, Nuala Bradley.
Front row: Claire McBride, Josephine O'Connor, Ursula McGee, Mary Sally, Eileen Meyler, Irene Courtney, Pat Stewart, Mary O'Neill, Rosaleen Gallagher, Bernadette McNally, Evelyn Dobbs, Eileen McBrearty, Noelle Bradley.

*Meet of Seskinore Harriers — c. 1910.*
*Extreme left: W. Edmund Orr.    Centre front: The Master Lewis I. Scott.    Next to the Master on the right is Andrew Leitch (Solicitor).*
*Second on right: Doctor Harpur.    Third on right: Ernest Orr.    Fourth on right: Fred Orr.*

*Seskinore House 1934*

Seskinore, the seat of Lieut.-Colonel John Knox McClintock, J.P., D.L., lies in the parish of Clogherny, near the village of Seskinore and Fintona, six miles south east of Omagh, Co. Tyrone. It stands in a park of 600 acres, and came into the possession of the family about a hundred years ago. The McClintock family are of Scotch origin, having settled in Ireland, 1597, from Argyll. Newtown House, Co. Louth, was the family place of this branch of McClintocks. The place having been sold the family came to live at Seskinore, which they inherited from the Perry family.

The Perry family is of Welsh origin, and their original patronymic was Perry, a James Perry being granted free farm lands from Sir Audley Mervyn in 1662. His eldest son, Francis, married a daughter of John Lowry, of Pomeroy, from whom descend the Earls of Belmore. The estates fell to the third son, George, who married a daughter of the Rev. James Sinclair, of Holyhill. His grandson, George, dying without issue, the estates passed to his nephew, Samuel, second son of his sister, Mary, who in 1781 married Alexander McClintock, of Newtown, Co. Louth, younger brother of John McClintock, of Drumcar, ancestor of Lord Rathdonnell. Samuel was a Lieutenant in the 18th Royal Irish Regiment, and High Sheriff of Co. Louth, and his eldest son, George Perry McClintock, Colonel who commanded 4th Royal Enniskilling Fusiliers (Royal Tyrone Fusiliers), was A.D.C. to the Duke of Abercorn and Earl Spencer when Lords Lieutenant, also J.P. and D.L. for Co. Tyrone, and High Sheriff in 1865. He married a daughter of the Rev. Samuel Alexander, of Termon, Co. Tyrone, whose wife was a daughter of the Rev. Charles Cobbe Beresford, Rector of Termon, a connection of the Marquess of Waterford, and his second son is the present owner of Seskinore.

Lieut.-Colonel McClintock's wife is a descendant of an old Scottish family of Eccles and Blakes, of Castlegrove, Co. Mayo. Settled in Ireland in 1600, from lands in the Barony of Eccles, Dumfrieshire.

The Seskinore Hunt, under that title, dates from 1886. It was previously known as the Tyrone Hunt, and was established in 1860 by the late Colonel George Perry McClintock, J.P., D.L., of Seskinore. He held the Mastership until 1886, when he was succeeded by his son, the present owner of Seskinore, Captain, now Lieut.-Colonel J. Knox McClintock, who re-named the Hunt, and retired in 1905. Mr. King Houston, of Riversdale, Omagh, was Master from 1905 to 1908; the present Master is Mr. Lewis Scott, of Omagh. These hounds meet twice a week. The country is undulating with bogs in parts which make hunting difficult, but south it is as good as any in the North of Ireland.

Extract from Pike's Province of Ulster 1909.

*Seskinore Harriers — Hunt Ball Meet 1931 at Camowen Crossroads.*
*From left: J. Dryden, S. O'Shiel, W. Orr, H. McCoy, Iris Moriarty, W. Taylor, H. Mark, D. Dobbs, B. Somerville, The Master Col. McClintock.*
*Note the dogs collared together to keep them from running away out of control.*

*Seskinore Hunt 1934. Hounds being released from their kennels to be fed.*

47

*One of Omagh's first petrol tankers, a Dennis owned by BP and driven by Robert Crane. Seen here sitting astride Killyclogher Bridge. Note the solid tyres. The workmen are using wooden props to stabilise the vehicle as there were no cranes available in 1930.*

*8 Campsie Road, the home of Harry Torney, one of Omagh's most able motor engineers. His garage was at the back of the house before he moved to the Dublin Road in 1938. Note McAleer's Campsie Bar and John McCrea's shop. John Curneen, whose wife owned this row of houses, lived in No. 6.*

*When W. 'Bonzo' Donnellan crashed his large open-tourer at the Dublin Road bridge it looked like this in 1938.*

*Some months later, without his right leg, he surveys his vehicle in Harry Torney's yard. He lived and drove a car for many years afterwards.*

*Hannan's chauffeur-driven taxis operated in the 1930's from the family home on the Derry Road. Dick Crawford is seen here with his Ford saloon JI4419. The barrack wall which runs along the right-hand side of the Derry Road is in the background.*

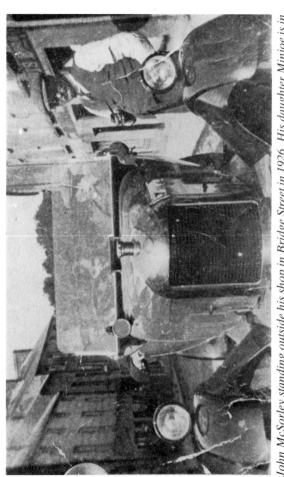

*John McSorley standing outside his shop in Bridge Street in 1926. His daughter Minjoe is in the middle of the front seat of the bull-nosed Morris.*

*Michael F. McSorley, 1908-1960, Omagh's most successful motor-cyclist on his 249 c.c. Rudge.*

*T. W. Guy, Dromore (346 Excelsior) and W. H. Neilands, Omagh (249 Rudge) were also regular competitors.*

# 1934 International North~West "200."

## THE AWARDS AND WINNERS.

**500 c.c. Class.**

| | | |
|---|---|---|
| J. Guthrie — Norton | Londonderry Trophy, Replica and £10. | 80.31 m.p.h. 2 hr. 28 min. 49.2 sec. |
| J. S. E. Mott — Rudge | Replica, and £6. | 76.75 — 2. 2.35.50 |
| J. H. White — Norton | Replica, and £3. | 74.89 — 3. 2.37.71 |

**350 c.c. Class.**

| | | |
|---|---|---|
| W. F. Rusk — Abbott | Coleraine Trophy, Replica and £10. | 73.66 m.p.h. 2.42.25 |
| F. G. O'Neill — Velocette | Replica, and £6. | 71.97 — 2. 2.46.11 |
| H. Pennington — Norton | Replica, and £3. | 71.13 — 3. 2.48.7 |

**250 c.c. Class.**

| | | |
|---|---|---|
| Mrs. McSorley — Rudge | Portrush Trophy, Replica and £10. | 66.69 m.p.h. 2.59.21 |
| W. Rebson — Dunelt | Replica, and £6. | 65.00 — 2. 3.4.0 |
| J. Duncan — N. Imperial | Replica, and £3. | 64.97 — 3. 3.4.5 |

Manufacturers' Team Award ... The N.W. "200" Trophy.

Club Team *(Club Medals to Riders).* Rusk, Moffat & McSorley

Fastest Lap. 500 Guthrie 8.5 sec. 82.15 350 Rusk 8.42 75.65 250 Rusk 9.28

Lap Leaders. 500 Guthrie 350 Guthrie 250 Benny Mart... 70.12

*(Replicas to Winners in each Class.)*

## GRAND OPEN HANDICAP.

*(All Competitors eligible.)*

1. M. Rebson — Dunelt ... The N.W. "200" Trophy, Replica and £12. 47 min.
2. F. G. O'Neill — Velocette ... Replica and £6. 19 min.
3. J. Guthrie — Norton ... Replica and £3. 29.

**Fastest Time on Handicap,** Confined to Private Entrants (other than First Prize Winners).

| | |
|---|---|
| 500 c.c. Class J. H. White — Norton | Perpetual Castlerock Cup. |
| 350 c.c. Class F. G. O'Neill — Velocette | Perpetual Portstewart Cup. |
| 250 c.c. Class J. Duncan — N. Imperial | Perpetual Ballymoney Cup. |

Confined Event ... The N.W. "200" Cup and Replica, and £3.

Competitor covering the 200 miles in fastest time, the said Competitor not having won a First, Second, or Third Prize in this or any other Open Road Race.

## Presentation of Prizes for the North-West "200"

In the "TROCADERO," PORTRUSH. The Prizes will be presented at 7.30 o'clock p.m. by Mrs. UTTERSON, wife of Lieut.-Colonel A. T. Le M. UTTERSON, D.S.O., Officer Commanding 2nd Battalion The Leicestershire Regiment, Londonderry.

**NOTE.**—Trophies in Scratch, Handicap, and Team Events to be held for ONE YEAR.

*From 1935 N.W. 200 Programme.*

*A motor rally starting outside the Belfast Bank in High Street in 1927 — starter Michael McSorley. Fancy rallying one of those large cars?*
*Early rallies were run under the auspices of the Omagh Motor and Motor-cycle Club — they parted company in 1929 and went their*
*separate ways. The Motor Club has survived without a break and is still one of the strongest supported motor clubs in Ulster.*

*Omagh Motor Club Directors, 1962.*
*Back row: Harry Reilly, —, Harry Johnston (D), Gordon Currie, Jim Rankin, P. J. Winters, Wm. Saulters, Kenneth Graham, Peter Johnston, Mervyn Armstrong.*
*Front row: John McAleer (D), Robin English, Ivan Allen (D), James Hunt, Dr. Haldane Mitchell.*
*The Club holds its monthly meetings in the Campsie Bar and has done for the past fifty years.*

*During the rail strike of 1933 a train was maliciously derailed at the Lynn Bridge. This photograph shows the Hall family who lived at King James' Bridge doing what all children would do on such an occasion.*
*From left: Jim Hall, Bertie Stevenson, Miss Gertrude Hall and Sam Hall.*

*'The Heather Queen' JI4935, a well-known Omagh bus which usually ran between Omagh and Cookstown via Gortin. In 1933 during the rail strike it was on loan to Billy Simpson for use on the Enniskillen route. Seen here with its driver, William Hawthorne from Broomehedge, Portadown, and his wife-to-be Miss Elizabeth McCormick of Cavanacaw. Billy drove the bus during the rail strike and later returned to his usual job as a railway engine driver. He went to live in Enniskillen and had eight children.*

*Charlie Mills Confectionery and Tobacconists in Market Street (1948) had one of the most eye-catching shop fronts in Omagh, with its beautiful tiled exterior, attributed to none other than John James Hall, builder of some repute in the 1920's and 1930's. The shop was owned and run by Jack Rossi over the war years until 1952 when it was acquired by neighbours Ita and Bridie Mullan.*

*Charlie Mills' van was an Austin 7 car given the new body in 1928 by who other than Harry Torney, Snr.*

*The Hardware House, 64 Market Street, was founded in 1910 by Mr. C. A. Anderson and his brother George, who later purchased 56 Market Street and traded there in grocery and provisions until the shop was demolished in 1966 to make way for Drumragh Avenue. The total frontage extended for 125 feet and from front to back 120 feet. The business is continued by Albert Martin who holds agencies for a number of well-known manufacturers and covers a complete range of domestic and furnishing ironmongery. The glass awning was a feature of the frontage until the early 1970's when terrorist action removed it in a few seconds.*

# 'Mat Mulcaghey'

*Wilson Guy (Mat Mulcaghey), 1875-1959, was born in Mullinagoagh, Dromore.*

*In 1893 aged 18 he went to the U.S.A., got a job as a draper — found the work too hard and came home in 1894.*

*He became a creamery manager, a radio ham, broadcaster and journalist.*

*His column in the Tyrone Constitution, 'What Now?' spanned 40 years. If it was all put together it would give a very interesting history of Omagh and its people over the years, being written in the dialect of the period.*

## THE CHILDHER THAT'S AWAY

I'm sitting by the ingle, the flure's swept nate and clane;
I'm feelin' quare and lonely — ye know the way I mane.
An' she looks quare and pensive, the morrow's Christmas Day;
Sure both of us bees thinkin' of the childher that's away.

Alas! We cuddent keep them, an' wan by wan they went,
I trust they're better done for, an' happy and content.
Sure, poverty's poor "kitchen", regard it as you may;
But still we can't help thinkin' of the childher that's away.

Wee Mat, an' Tam an' Mary are in a farrin' lan'.
An' her an' me jist struggles, to do the best we can.
I hope they're well an' happy, God sen' them luck the day;
For I might niver see them — them childher that's away.

I'm gettin' oul' an' donsey, an' she's not much behine;
For all her faults and failin's she has a heart that's kine.
An' some day soon, I'm thinkin' we'll lay the besoms by,
An' her and me'll be headin' for mansions in the sky.

Full often by yon portals both her and me will stray
In eagerness to welcome the childher that's away.

EMPIRE DAY. OMAGH 1924. THE SOUNDING OF THE OLD REVEILLE
PROCEEDS OF SALE IN AID OF OMAGH MODEL SCHOOL AND BOY SCOUTS
WEMBLEY FUND

*Empire Day, 1924. The sounding of the Old Reveille. It is interesting to note that H. Mawhinney's plumbing and sanitary engineers' shop has been demolished to make way for the Munster and Leinster Bank.*

**The Rev. Brother Hamill's Choir of the late thirties, Feis prizewinners on many occasions.**

Back row (left to right): Rev. Fr. J. McElholm, W. Laird, J. Nixon, Rev. Fr. T. Bennett, E. McNaboe, D. Cullen, P. McGartland, W. Breslin, C. Bowes, J. McCullagh, B. Gillespie, J. McCaffrey, J. McCrossan, — Bell, R. Campbell, B. Cox, P. McCaul, J. Hynes, K. Murnaghan, F. Curneen, L. George.

Fourth row (left to right): J. Mellon, H. McBride, P. Haughey, E. McCaffrey, T. McElhinney, L. McCrumlish, T. Cassidy, J. McCann, — Brennan, E. Doake, J. O'Neill, — Brennan, C. Mullin, T. McCann, B. O'Reilly — Mannion, F. Teague.

Third row (left to right): J. Doherty, D. Bowes, M. McGread, G. McGonigle, ——, S. Noble, F. McGirr, — Donaghey, T. McGartland, M. Corry, Rev. S. Cunningham, H. O'Neill, E. McLaughlin, T. Gallagher, M. Vaughan, I. O'Reilly, C. Doake, O. Mooney.

Second row (left to right): J. McCausland, J. Hickey, J. Kirwin, J. Gormley, J. Lynn, T. O'Reilly, T. Sweeney, Rev. P. Cunningham, J. Cunningham, H. Scully, H. Hunt, P. Scully, Rev. Fr. J. Boyle, C. Hunter, T. Mathers, — Bell, Rev. Bro. H. McKinney, M. Cox.

Front row (left to right): S. Young, J. Bradley, E. McCanny, F. Cox, G. Hamilton, B. Mullan, ——, G. McGovern, J. Fisher, L. McCusker, F. McGahern, P. Donnelly, ——, B. McCann, P. McGeown.

*The Rev. Brother Hamill in a relaxed mood at the C.B.S. sports ground at Mountjoy Road in the late 1930's. He was an enthusiastic musician and sportsman — his brother Michael played soccer for Belfast Celtic. Most of all he will be remembered by many Omagh boys for setting them out on the road to successful professional careers world-wide.*

*Omagh Choral Society — 1956.*

*Formed in the 1950's by Jack Anderson, they performed regularly in the County Cinema with visiting guest stars like Isobel Baillie (1954), Derek Bell, Dr. Havelock Nelson, Tom Davidson, Owen Brannigan (1958), Patricia Varley (1960), David Galliver (1961) and Robin Hall and Jimmie MacGregor (1962).*

*Sopranos — Mesdames M. A. Allen, A. Bann, G. P. Bann, M. F. Bann, E. C. Clements, Enid Collins, Evelyn Collins, O. Ingram, P. M. Kelso, M. S. Laird, H. M. Logan, D. McMichael, J. M. A. McKinley, N. McMillen, F. E. Mulligan, B. M. Price, J. Robinson, C. A. Simpson, F. M. Stephens, A. E. J. Walker.*

*Contraltos — Mesdames M. Adams, E. P. Coote, F. K. Corrigan, A. Donaghy, E. A. Holmes, M. E. Mitchell, M. P. Mitchell, M. Monteith, E. G. Pierce, A. Roy, K. I. Smith.*

*Tenors — S. Davidson, R. A. Elliott, W. J. Greer, R. Haire, W. Harte, T. McMichael, A. Thompson, R. Walker, R. J. White.*

*Basses — R. Allsop, T. S. Birrell, R. A. Black, J. Bowman, W. H. Conn, T. Gilliland, R. J. Hadden, B. McCord, J. E. Preston, A. Simmons, C. Snell, H. Williamson.*

*Accompanist — Mrs. M. J. Simpson.*

*During the 1950's and 1960's Rotarian Paddy Laird wrote and acted in eleven pantomimes in Omagh Town Hall. The script was fluid and had to be changed each night to refer to members of the audience. The photograph shows Frank Ball and Paddy Laird as the Ugly Sisters in 'Cinderella' (both smoking! — fancy).*

*When Brother T. A. Burke was Superior of the Christian Brothers School from 1928-1934 the pupils played rugby — trained by the late Tony Shannon. The above team reached the semi-finals of the Ulster Schools Cup in 1933/34 only to be beaten by R.B.A.I. 8-0 in the last ten minutes of the game, which was played at the Omagh Christian Brothers Park.*

*Back row: Gerry McEnhill, Omagh, retired principal (centre threequarters at St. Mary's, Strawberry Hill); Fr. Tom O'Kane, a priest in Australia (he had a trial for Ulster); Michael Scully (deceased); Harry Torney, Jnr., Omagh (deceased); Jim McVeigh (was in the Under 15's and came in at full-back against R.B.A.I.); Harry O'Hagan (was full back at St., Mary's, Strawberry Hill); Mr. Tony Shannon (Manager and Teacher).*

*Centre row: J. J. McElholm, Trillick, retired principal; Frank Monaghan, Fintona, retired principal teacher; Jim McWilliams, teacher (deceased); Paddy Donnelly, Trillick, retired principal teacher; Malachy McAleer, retired principal; Dick Minnis, lived at 2 Mountjoy Terrace, Omagh (a teacher who went to Ceylon and became a tea planter); John McCarroll, Fintona.*

*Front row: Dermot McMahon, became a priest (deceased) and Benny Rafferty, still living at Woodside Terrace, Omagh.*

*Omagh Academicals R.F.C., founded in 1952 and adopted the name from the grammar school. The 'Accies' (as they are known throughout Ulster and beyond) were founded by the late Billy Beatty, Tom Hendly and Dai Waterson. They play at the Thomas Mellon Playing Fields at Coneywarren, acquired in 1967 with the help of a grant from Dr. Matthew T. Mellon, of the banking firm in Pittsburgh. The Mellon ancestral home is at the Ulster-American Folk Park nearby.*

*1st XV 1954-55*

*Back row: Wm. Beatty (deceased), A. Ballantine, Sam Hammond, Maurice Bloomfield, Phil Richardson, Kyle Mulligan (played for Ulster), Dai Waterson, Harry McCartney.*
*Front row: Norman Gilpin, Derek Dunn, D. Houston, H. A. (Biro) Kerr, Billy Charleton, John Devlin (deceased).*

*Omagh Rugby Football Club XV 1931-32, winners of the McMillin Cup.*
*Back row: J. Campbell, S. Hill, D. Christie, W. J. W. Donaldson, T. W. Guy, J. R. McMillin.*
*Middle row: Mr. Joseph McMillin, J. Gunn, J. S. Campbell, J. L. Baxter, J. A. Cotter, Captain B. Gosselin, R.M. (President).*
*Front row: N. R. J. Wilson, G. A. Maginnis, E. J. Pettit (Captain), J. J. Pollock.*

*Silver salver presented to N. R. J. Wilson by Omagh Rugby Football Club on the occasion of his marriage, 25th July, 1934.*

*Signed by (clockwise):*
*P. J. Smith, P. McAlinney, J. McGale,*
*W. H. Neilands, H. M. Mark,*
*J. M. McMillin, E. J. Pettit,*
*G. A. Maginnis, James Campbell,*
*T. W. Guy, F. McGale,*
*W. H. Kempston, J. O'Doherty,*
*J. Gunn, E. Isdell, A. Bell, J. R. Pollock,*
*W. J. Mullan, J. R. McMillin,*
*S. S. Wilson, Maurice French.*

*The first motorised hearse in Omagh was owned by John Porter of High Street. It was a Ford — registration number JI 2654 — seen here outside St. Columba's Parish Church in the 1920's. Note it has pneumatic tyres. The lorry sitting opposite is also a Ford — registration number JI 1633.*

*Drumragh School 1933.*
*Back row: Joe Knox, — Thompson, William Porter, Fred Wright, William Lowry, Tom Knox, Drew Wright, Sam Robinson, Jim McCrea.*
*Middle row: Eliz. Newell, Alphonsus Tracey, Jim McKimmon, Rachel McKimmon, Evelyn Barry, Eliz. McAshea, Sarah McKelvey, Nora McKelvey, Eliz. Lowry, Annie Clements, Sarah Mitchell, Eric Porter, Sarah Newell (teachers were sisters).*
*Front row: Anthony Knox, William Clements, Hugh Campbell, Norman Robinson, Harold Robinson, —, Ruth Foster, Eccles Foster, — McCutcheon, Mabel McCrea, Eliz. Beattie, Peggy Robinson.*

*Omagh Model School Choir c. 1930, ready to set off to Dungannon Feis.*
*Back row: William Woods, Bertie Newell, Joe Graham, Joe Gray, Willie Woods, Fraser Walsh, R. A. McMaster (Head of Sion Mills P.S.).*
*Second row: Daisy Allen, ——, — Mathews, Daisy Hamilton, Marion Smith, Jean Hopper, ——, — Graham.*
*Front row: Peggy Davison, Lena McKimmon, — McCollum, Betty Adams, Gladys Fallows, — McMichael, Jean Faux, Pearl Rodgers, Irene Alcorn.*

*This winter scene of Omagh was taken by amateur photographer Jim Mills (deceased), who worked in Scotts Mill for many years, from where this photograph was taken c. 1950. The County Hall has not yet been built, the Model School is still there and the pylon in the middle of the skyline is at the rear of the R.U.C. Station in High Street.*

*The Police Station in Omagh had many sites in the main street before ending up on the Mountjoy Road in the early 1960's. The site remembered by most is where Broderick's Health Studio and the Dragon Castle Restaurant is today. This photograph taken on V.E. Day, May 1945, shows from left to right: Sgt. John Hughes, Constable King, Constable McKinley, Sgt. McKibbin and Constable J. Roberts.*

*The arrival of the Judge for the Assizes was always a big attraction. He is seen here arriving in Pollock's Rolls Royce with Jimmy Reilly at the wheel and Robert Crawford doorman, in 1944. He would inspect a guard of honour drawn up from the regiment resident at Lisanelly Barracks. He would usually dine in the County Club and in the early days he would sleep there as well. In the early years of this century a Judge from Dublin passed away in his sleep in the County Club. Note the Melville Hotel in the background which was owned by a Miss Robinson. It wasn't a large hotel, but she also owned 'Clonavon' on the Hospital Road which she used as an overflow when required.*

*This aerial view of Omagh in the mid 1940's shows no development north of the town, but many places that have since disappeared are still easily visible. For example starting at the top left, the Dromore Road single-storeyed houses, McGaghey's Row are easily seen. Behind the Station 'Ashfield House' sits out on its own. Starrs Crescent is in the course of erection. The Steam Laundry chimney is clearly visible; it was behind what is Rotarian M. J. O'Kane's premises today. The gardens below were behind Henderson's Foundry and the small house below the Laundry was occupied by Amy Henderson, sister of Robert Henderson. The large house on the left is 'Bellevue', once lived in by Frank Crawford of Crawford & Wilson's; the site today is occupied by the Christian Brothers School. Further down the left side, the first houses of Johnston Park can be seen, but there is no development between them and Scarffe's Entry. At the bottom of the Academy playing field is a small pavilion that ended up at Campsie, but the Preparatory Department hasn't yet been built. Spiller's House is seen to the left of Torney's Garage, while Eakin's Garage has not yet been built. At the bottom of the photograph is the Market Yard Goods Depot where the new Library stands today. The roofs of Spiller's Place are just visible in the lower left corner.*

# ⤜ Faces from the Past ⤛

**PETER McGOVERN.**
On stage his talents would
have graced a West End
career.

**GEORGE PENTLAND.**
Motor mechanic who kept
Gortin's vehicles mobile for
many years, including my
father's.

**DAN McBRIDE.**
Turf accountant in Omagh
for over 50 years.

**WILLIS SHEFFIELD.**
Jeweller and talented amateur
photographer. Enthusiastic
golfer — he even played in
the snow (with coloured golf
balls!).

**SAM STEELE.**
His name was linked to the
bicycle business for many
years.

**PETE McANENA.**
Without his taxi Mountfield
would have been cut off
from the outside world.

*When Lawrence's photographer Bob French came to Omagh in the 1880's he took a photograph of Campsie Crescent with the Orange Hall in the background — he called it Sandy Row. This 12th of July Arch on Campsie Bridge in 1938 was made by the residents of Campsie Avenue and Campsie Crescent. The Somerville brothers Ernie and Jack are seen in the middle. When the bridge was widened no arch was erected for many years. Now Mountfield L.O.L. erects an arch in July each year across the Swinging Bars roundabout.*

*Lower Market Street in 1950 below Campsie Bridge, erected 1836. This photograph was taken before the bridge was widened and shows on the left: Peter Smith's, Bob Booth's (Hairdresser), Miss Devlin's and McCann's. On the right is McGuigan's (Plumbing Contractors), where Charlie Allen is today.*

*The Victoria Cafe in 1929 run by Miss Miles, beside Phair's Shoe Shop; note the pairs of shoes hanging round the doorway. Traynor's mineral lorry is obstructing a view of the shop window. The man having trouble with the pig seems to bear out the American theory that we did keep pigs in our homes in the past. Well I can remember at least two houses in Campsie which kept pigs in their backyards. The Victoria Cafe later became Ronnie McKnight's Greengrocey Shop while Phair's became Jackson's and later William McIlveen's.*

*The staff and owners of Isaac Boyd & Sons, 1948.*
*From left to right: Liam Brogan, Rita McBride, Noreen McCrory (deceased), Catherine Sloane (deceased), Richard Sloane (deceased),*
*Lucy Armstrong, Gladys McCausland (née Graham), William Brandon.*

*A group of Omagh Solicitors preparing for their annual outing in the mid-1930's.*
*The group includes: Joseph Robinson (Clerk), Gerald Murnaghan, ——, Norman Holland, Fred Colhoun, Arthur Davison, Roderick O'Connor, Captain W. H. Fyffe, James McNulty, Albert Monteith.*

*St. Columba's Church Fête, 1931, held at Campsie.*

*Back row (standing): Mrs. McDougall, Mrs. Hendly, Mrs. Beattie, Violet Wilton, Patricia Moore (née Hamilton), Mr. Ward, Diana Dobbs (holding pony), Rev. O'Neile, Col. Dobbs, Mrs. Jordan.*

*3rd row (standing): Mrs. P. Richardson, Phil Richardson (boy), R. T. Newell, George Anderson, Mrs. Donnelly, Mrs. Anderson, Margaret Kerr, Mrs. McKinley, Mrs. Cadden, Miss Moriarty, Mrs. Hamilton, Mrs. Rodgers, Mrs. de la Ray, Nelson Rountree.*

*2nd row (seated): ——, Mrs. Blake, Miss E. Ward, ——, Mrs. Hamilton, Canon Cullimore, Mrs. Rountree, Miss Moore, Mrs. Ingram, ——.*

*Kneeling: Barbara Hull, Mattie Cummings, Jean McCausland, Jean Hamilton, Annie Fenton, Sarah Buchanan, Isobel Anderson.        Boys: Harold Warner, —, P. Evans.*

*In this the Centenary Year of the Church Lads' Brigade, here is the St. Columba's Company in 1933.*
*Back row (left to right): Noel Pigott, Sammy Johnston, Billy Carmichael, Herbie Kerr, Sam McConnell, Bob Pigott, Dick Wilton, Henry Moffitt, Willie Johnston, Bob Elliott, Jackie Cadden, Johnny McCrea, Jim McMichael.*
*2nd row (left to right): ——, ——, Willie Mehaffy, Willie McClelland, Tommy McMichael, B. Monteith, Jim Elliott, David Wylie, Jim Thompson, William Potts, Francis Mills.*
*3rd row (left to right): Eccles Foster, Gerry Henderson, Davy Baird, ——, Jack McCausland, Thomas Elliott, Col. Dobbs, Rev. Mee, Gordon Clarke, Willie McClelland, ——, ——, Tom Stewart.*
*Front row: ——, ——, Jackie Thompson, Norman Potts, Tommy Nixon.*

*St. Columba's Church Lads' Brigade, c. 1958.*

*Back row (left to right): Norman Campbell, Brian Wakely, Robert Hempton, Dale Robinson, Allen Retalic, Derek Shaw, Roger Fleming, Bobby Collins, William Gilmore, Billy Fulton, Roy Smith, Patrick Johnston, David Caldwell, Billy Campbell.*

*Third row (left to right): Russell Fleming, Freddie Hempton, Matt Smith, Leslie Patton, Noel Kerr, Derek Reid, Harold Robinson, Raymond Bann, Robin Wakely, Kenneth Kerr, Leslie Young.*

*Second row (left to right): John Ashenhurst, Alan Ashenhurst, Martin McMichael, Tommy McMichael, Canon Wakely, Dean Orr, Mr. Shaw, William Todd, Ramsey Allen.*

*Front row (left to right): Mervyn Camley, Richard Fulton, David Fulton, — Shaw, Ronald Kerr, Bill McCollum, Ross McCausland.*

*The King George V Jubilee in 1935 was celebrated in Campsie in a manner never seen before or since. Sandy Row (Campsie Avenue and Campsie Crescent) was dressed overall with flags and bunting, which was paid for by the residents themselves, paying 1 penny per household per week for many weeks. The ladies of the street, ably led by Mrs. Wilton, made all the bunting themselves and bought the Union Flags. The price of all the decorations seen in these two photographs amounted to £25 in all.*

*The decorations in Campsie Avenue for the King George V Jubilee in 1935 and the organising committee.*
*Left to right: Tom Colvin, Bob Kinloch, Marcus Pigott, Ernest Cummings, Robert Lynn, Mervyn Lynn (boy), Gordon Clarke, John Moffitt, Jim Moffitt (boy), Joe Monteith,*
*Dick Wilton, Ira Love, Harry Nixon.*

*Thomas Johnston leading the Children's Parade along Market Street on Coronation Day, 12th May, 1937. The parade is passing the present-day Northern Bank. Note the properties opposite have all changed hands since then — Charles V. McAleer's, Central Hotel and licensed premises; W. T. Quigley's garage with its unique petrol pump with five globes; Crawford & Crawford, the drapers; McGinn's (family grocers) and McAleer's cycle shop.*

*1st Omagh Boys' Brigade Pipe Band led the Children's Day Parade in 1937. This is the band in the early 1930's.*
*Back row: Jim Carson, Tommy Woods, Dick Wilton, D. (Dutchie) Speers, Jay Pollock, Fred Farren, Willie Johnston.*
*Front row: James Cathcart, Vivian McFarland, Ernie McMichael, Albert McCutcheon, Sam Hall, William Greer, Jim McGrew.*

*Patrick Farrell* *(1856-1938), the poet, was born in the townland of Shantavney, Ballygawley (better known today as Ballymacilroy). He married a local girl, Isabella McFadden, and they raised a family of thirteen children. His poems are about life and nature in the surrounding area where he lived. If you turn to the right at the bottom of Ballymacilroy Hill you enter the Glencull Waterside with all its beauty and tranquillity, far removed from the pace of life that flows to and fro at speed on the main road of the 1990's.*

## GLENCULL WATERSIDE

'Tis pleasant for to take a stroll,
  By Glencull Waterside,
On a lovely evening in Spring,
  In Nature's early pride.
You will pass by many a flowery bank,
  And many a fertile dell,
Like walkin' through enchanted land,
  Where fairies used to dwell.

The trout is rising to the fly,
  The lambkins sport and play,
And the pretty feathered warblers
  Are singing by the way.
While the blackbirds' and thrushes' notes
  By the echoes multiplied,
They fill the vale with melody
  By Glencull Waterside.

Show not to me the headlands bold,
  That mock the oceans' waves,
Nor the mountainous waves careering
  Among the ocean caves.
But show to me the fertile vales,
  The farmers' joy and pride,
Where blossomed orchards sweetly bloom,
  By Glencull Waterside.

Here verdant fields and gentle slopes,
  Enriched besparkling rills,
When clothed in Summer's flowery garb,
  The heart with pleasure fills.
If Avoca's vale does not prevail,
  That is the poet's pride,
Let sweet Adare its glories share,
  With Glencull Waterside.

Give not to me the rugged scenes,
  Of which some love to write,
Of beetling cliffs o'er hanging crags,
  And the eagle in its flight.
But give to me the fertile fields,
  The farmers' joy and pride,
With homestead and the orchards fine
  Like Glencull Waterside.

These scenes bring recollections back,
  Of comrades scattered wide,
Who used to walk along these banks,
  In youthful manly pride.
And maidens fair, who free from care
  Sailed o'er the billows wide,
And left fond hearts to mourn their loss,
  By Glencull Waterside.

'Tis sad to think of lives oft spent
  In many a foreign land,
In search of fabled rivers that
  Roll on golden sand;
Some lose their health in search of wealth
  By fortune oft denied,
Who might have lived in sweet content
  By Glencull Waterside.

The sparkling diamonds of the Rhand,
  Or Klondyke's shining ore,
But ill repays the withered heart
  That worships such a stone.
Many blessings grace this beauteous place,
  'Tis here I would reside,
We have peace and health and honest wealth
  By Glencull Waterside.

*The Rev. Tyndall John Willoughby, Rector of Gortin, in his 14 h.p. Darrecq (Tonneau, green 21 cwt.), first registered on 18th January, 1911 — Registration number JI 195. Miss Emily Willoughby behind the wheel was the first woman in Co. Tyrone to hold a driving licence.*

*Omagh's position, surrounded by mountains and moorland, has always been an attractive area for outdoor field sports. The Ulster Irish Red Setter Club was formed at Balmoral, Belfast, on the 23rd July, 1908, and officially registered with the Kennel Club in August of the same year. They held their meetings in the Grand Metropole Hotel in York Street for many years until P. J. O'Callaghan (the then Manager of Omagh Gas Works, and a keen field sportsman) persuaded the Club in 1926 to have Omagh as its headquarters, and since then the Club's Trials have each year been held in the third week of July on the moors around Omagh. This photograph taken on the Pigeon Top in July 1950 shows two of the Club's foremost members. On the left, Vincent Courtney, still an active member, and fourth from the left, Fred Colhoun (deceased), who was Chairman for many years.*

*This photograph taken in May 1942 shows P. J. O'Callaghan, on the left, with his four Lakeland terriers. He is showing the kill of the 30th and 31st May to T. R. G. Patterson, the Manager of the Provincial Bank. Seventeen foxes and badgers in all. The local farmers, if they had a problem with badgers or foxes, would send for P. J. O'Callaghan or some of his friends who were experts with their dogs in dealing with what the farmers called vermin. It was not unusual for P. J. O'Callaghan's dogs to kill over one hundred foxes and badgers in a season.*

*Angela and Patricia Eaton, daughters of Arthur Eaton, the then Consultant Surgeon at the Tyrone County Hospital, and a friend with their pointers on the Pigeon Top in July 1950, waiting for the Trials to begin. The straps over their shoulders are their binoculars. Note in the background the sweeping moorland down towards Omagh.*

*The Club trophies are quite unique in quality especially the three silver claret jugs (similar to the British Open Golf Championship Trophy). Bill Hosick (centre) made history in 1990 when he won all three stakes at the same trial — the first time this has been achieved.*

*Rhu Gorse (468 44), winner of the Ulster Gundog Trial in 1926. The Red Setter was owned by Mr. W. J. Patterson (County Executive Officer in Agriculture in Tyrone). Her success was such that a cup is named in her memory.*

*Between the wars, Omagh had its own Greyhound Track in the Showgrounds. It was managed by Paddy Keenan, a Greencastle man who lived at 24 Campsie Road. This photograph taken in 1936 by Willis Sheffield clearly shows a portion of the track in the left-hand side through the trees.*

# Tyrone County Coursing Club

### (UNDER I.C.C. RULES).

## ~ COURSING ~

— AT —

## STRATHROY HOLM, OMAGH,

— ON —

## WEDNESDAY, 26th DECEMBER, 1934.

### First Brace in Slips at 11 o'clock, sharp.

Judge—Mr. J. FULLERTON.     Slipper—Mr. G. CAMPBELL.

PRESIDENT—HIS GRACE THE DUKE OF ABERCORN.

CHAIRMAN OF COMMITTEE—JAMES CAMPBELL, Esq.

PATRONS—Rt. Hon. Earl of Belmore, D.L.; Rt. Hon. Earl of Enniskillen, K.P., D.L.; R. Dixon Anderson, Esq.; John Collum, Esq., D.L.; James Campbell, Esq.; Dr. J. A. Cunningham, F. B. Foerster, Esq.; Dr. Bernard Lagan, Henry Mussen, Esq.; Daniel M'Sorley, Esq., J.P.; Francis O'Shiel. Esq.; Joseph Shaw, Esq.

STIPENDARY STEWARD—J. M'Guigan.

FIELD STEWARDS—James Campbell, D. Barbour, P. J. O'Callaghan.

CALL STEWARDS—L. M'Closkey, A. M'Cready, M. Hunt, S. Gormley, H. Johnston, T. Pritchard, B. M'Aleer.

FLAG STEWARD—George Beatty.

SLIP STEWARD—Felix Teague.

HON. VETERINARY SURGEONS—E. Johnston, T. Dunn.

TREASURER—Dr. J. A. Cunningham.

P. KEENAN, Hon. Sec., Omagh.

## PROGRAMMES: - - 1/- EACH.

### ADMISSION TO GROUNDS, 2/4 (Including Tax).

### LUNCHEONS SERVED ON FIELD.

*The Tyrone County Coursing Club held regular meetings at Strathroy Holm. The front of this programme for Boxing Day 1934 lists the Club officials, quite a few of them with Omagh connections.*

*A group at a coursing meeting at Strathroy Holm in the 1930's. Jack Devlin is in the centre of the front row. In the background are the tall trees of the Rash Estate, previously part of the Mountjoy Forest, at one time one of the largest forests in Ireland, and owned by the Blessingtons, who lived in Mountjoy Castle (Old Mountjoy today).*

*Spillers Place in July 1936. The lady standing at the door was a Mrs. Taylor. The garages on the right of the photograph originally housed Omagh's first fire engine (motorised) and later the Post Office Telephone vehicles. It is now roadway. Spillers Place was demolished in 1966. It is now the site of Omagh's new Library.*

*Torney's Garage on the Dublin Road was built in 1938 and was the first purpose-built garage in Omagh. Harry Torney, Snr., originally had his premises in Campsie Avenue, where Campsie Court is today. He was a motor engineer ahead of his time and during the 2nd World War when parts were unobtainable his skill with the lathe saw many a car remain on the road with parts manufactured by his own hands. This photograph was taken by Norman Anderson in 1947; in fact, Norman is seen here setting off in his Vauxhall for a tour of France and Switzerland.*

*The interior of Torneys' garage in 1938 shortly after it had opened. This amazing sight shows that few cars in those days had hard tops. Considering it rains on an average of 270 days out of the 365 in Omagh, I doubt if these Fords and Austins were particularly comfortable to drive in.*

*Omagh Girl Guides at Trinity in early 1930's.*
*Back row (left to right): Margaret Kerr, ——, Maggie Hamilton, Audrey Donaghy, Betty Lyons, Jean Charleton, Carrie Farren.*
*Middle row (left to right): ——, Beatrice Mitchell, Monica Orr, Miss R. E. Fyffe (Assistant Captain), Miss Norah McAdam (Captain), Vivienne Adrain, Isobel Pigott.*
*Front row (left to right): Florrie Fowler, Tillie Hamilton, Denise White, Daisy Hamilton, Doreen McCrea, Dorothy McKillop, Gladys Fallows, Beatrice Alcorn.*

*Omagh Boy Scouts c. 1948.*
*Back row (left to right): D. B. T. Scott, Mrs. R. H. Ellis, Colin McMeekin, John Burke, John Robinson, Sammy Hezlett, R. R. Hifle (Manager, Bank of Ireland).*
*Middle row (left to right): James (Jairus) Ballantine, Fred Richardson, ——, ——, Noel Preston.*
*Front row (left to right): Douglas Chambers, Tom Mansell, Sam Gallagher, Ronnie McCartney.*
*The Omagh Scouts have to thank the Ellis family of Rash over the years for giving them the facilities for camping on their estate.*

*Omagh Technical College has had several homes, starting in the Town Hall and moving to the present Academy site until the present Omagh College of Further Technology was built on the site of the old Model School. This is the staff on 8th June, 1957, at Sports Day.*

*Back row (left to right): Agnes Shorthall, Marie McKeone (née Collins), Maureen Fox, Hilda Breen (nèe Kerr), Jim Cowan (deceased), Dessie Flanagan.*
*Front row (left to right): Bob Craig (deceased), Mary Gallagher, Muriel McFarland, Mrs. Anne Lynch, P. J. Brennan (Principal) (deceased), Victor Cordner (Vice-Principal), Ada McConnell (deceased), Kenneth Collins, Edgar Weir (deceased).*

*Omagh Technical School Football Team, 1949.*
*Back row (left to right): Mr. O'Reilly, Douglas Bell, D. Rutledge (deceased), E. Quinn, Robin Crawford, George Rutledge, P. J. Brennan (Principal) (deceased).*
*Front row (left to right): J. Young, Raymond Harkness, S. Wilson, T. McClean, M. Kerr, J. McGuigan.*

The Gospel Hall, Dublin Road, is conducted by the Plymouth Brethren who have a large membership in the district. The Dublin Road assembly was planted in 1860 through the great revival of 1859. They met originally upstairs in Miss Spiller's School until the first hall was built in 1916 (as in photograph c. 1955). The hall was rebuilt in 1964-65 and has a seating capacity of 160.

*William McCracken, a staunch member of the Plymouth Brethren, had his forge in the Old Market Place, opposite Kevin McCormack's butcher's shop and behind William Todd's insurance agency. It looks very much today as it did in 1920 when the photograph was taken. William is on the left, the man shoeing the horse is Harry Armstrong and he went to Australia in 1924.*

*Omagh Model School Soccer Team, 1946.*
*Back row (left to right): A. Thompson, William Gilchrist, Roy Hannigan, Shane Chesney (deceased), David Gilchrist, Robin Crawford.*
*Front row (left to right): Douglas Bell, Billy Jebb, S. Wilson, T. Hughes, Cedric Shanks.*
*Playing record: lost to Technical School 1-2, drew with Technical School 1-1, drew with Technical School 2-2, beat Technical School 3-1, beat Technical School 5-1, beat Omagh Academy 1-0, beat Omagh Academy 17-2.*

*Omagh has always been a popular angling centre and still is, thanks to the good work carried out each year by the Omagh Anglers Association, who look after the local rivers and lakes and keep them stocked. Here are association members in Spillers Place in 1957 with fish fry from a Whiteabbey fish farm for stocking the local streams.*
*Back row (left to right): Lou Lynch, Jack McMillin, Dr. Hugh Watson, Capt. Maddin Scott, R. H. Holland, William Miller, R.M., R. McGuigan, J. McDonald, Thos. Hannigan, Ernest Allen, P. Cunningham, Joe Mathers, Bob Gray, Ernie Hamilton, J. Campbell.*
*Front row (left to right): Bobbie Lynn, William Davidson, Patrick Miller, George Murdock, Bobby Lambert.*

*Right: Circuit of Ireland official Bentham White and member of Omagh Motor Club, seeing Ronnie McCartney off on his four days of hard driving round Ireland to become the first member of Omagh Motor Club to win the event outright. Also in the photograph are Bill Dallas and Bill Wright of the Ministry of Agriculture (Forestry Division).*

*Below: One week later, Ronnie is seen with his Mini Cooper-S sitting on four Castrol oil drums in Charleton's Garage on the Derry Road, where he was a car salesman, with the winner's trophy.*

*This year with a similar car he won the Classic Cars Monte Carlo Rally outright, with another Omagh man Donal McBride in an Austin Healey '3000' (prepared by Nicholas Murray) fifth.*

*Little did Bob Crowe realise what he was starting when he suggested to the directors of Omagh Motor Club in the early 1950's that they should run a Hill Climb at Syonfin, near Fintona. The event flourished until 1978 when overheads made it impossible to continue. Although the name that springs to most people's mind is Tommy Reid from Tandragee, who had a popular series of wins in the 1970's, it is Patsy McGarrity of Alto Cars, Belfast, who still holds the record. He is seen in the photograph with Harry P. Johnston, the club's most popular secretary. McGarrity's time in the 1978 Tuborg sponsored event was 43·85 secs. in a Chevron B29 Formula Atlantic 1600 cc.*

*This Model T Ford was McMullan's first Calor Gas vehicle in Omagh. Seen here, in Drumragh Car Park with the Cenotaph and Orange Hall on the right. The Model School is on the left, in 1944. The van was driven by Billy Davidson who worked for the same firm for over 40 years.*

*This similar Ford van was J. B. Anderson's small furniture van, usually driven by George Burns (deceased). George was a man of many talents and will be remembered by Omagh children as J. B. Anderson's Santa Claus for years. One of his delights was to set up the Hornby train layout in the large shop window each Christmas and watch the little boys' eyes follow it round and round for long periods.*

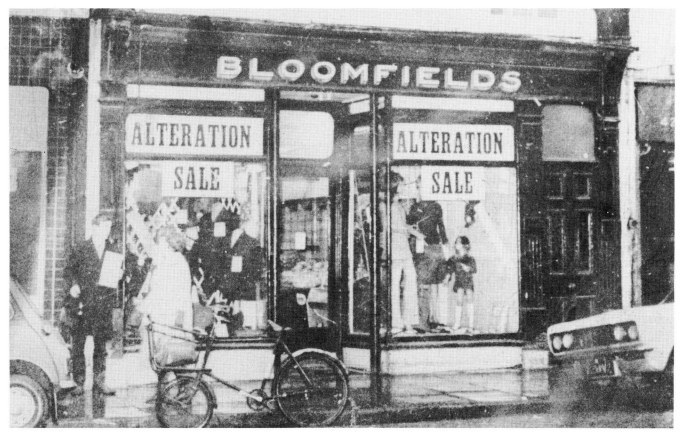

*Bloomfield's Shop in High Street seen here in 1950 before renovations. It was run by Rotarian Maurice Bloomfield and his wife Myrtle as a ladies' and gents' clothing store until the National and Provincial Building Society took over the ground floor in the early 1980's. Note the delivery bicycle propped against the kerb has a large parcel in its front rack.*

*The Premier Show Band.*
*During the war years there were several bands which entertained the locals and the troops in halls in and around the town. The Richardson brothers' Excelsior was popular as was the O.K. Showband, called after Oliver Kinloch who formed it originally. When Oliver went to the U.S.A. the band changed its name to the Premier Show Band. It is seen here playing in Mountjoy Orange Hall. From the left: Andy Hannigan (drums), Kenneth Kinloch (banjo), Willie Braiden (saxophone) and Cecil Kinloch (accordion).*

*During the war years entertainment parties were formed to entertain the troops. This group, mainly of members of the Y.M.C.A., have just been entertaining soldiers in St. Columba's Hall in 1940 when this photograph was taken.*
*Back row (left to right): Kenneth Crane (photographer), Bertie Parke.*
*Third row (left to right): Tommy Richardson, Phil Richardson, Ira Love, R. T. Newell, W. Dick, Victor Burr, ——.*
*Second row (left to right): Daisy Richardson, Tommy Strain, Ray Parke, Miss Quigley, Mrs. Burr, James Hamilton.*
*Front row (left to right): Bob McFadden and Mrs. McFadden and the six soldiers, four of whom were teenagers, were all killed at Dunkirk a short time later.*

*The 1960's saw the beginning of the Big Band era and, as a result, homes, garages and back sheds resounded to the many practising amateur budding musicians and up went the electricity bills. It is said that at one time Omagh had more bands than any other town of its size in Ireland. The Plattermen was one such band — 1965.*

*Back row (left to right): Johnny Murphy, Artie McGlynn, Pat Chesters, Sean Hamilton, Leo Doran and Ray Moore. Front row (left to right): Billy McGinty and Brian Coll. The success of this group is born out of the fact that Artie McGlynn has developed into one of the most versatile guitarists in Ireland. In no small measure has Pat Chesters kept Omagh's oldest band, the St. Eugene's Brass, still intact after 120 years. Ray Moore, a member of one of Omagh's most talented musical families, has his own group and is a multiple instrumentalist. Last but not least, Brian Coll, still singing with his own band — his voice has travelled the world on record and tape.*

*The Polka Dots, 1961.*
*Back row (left to right): Mickey Chesters, Charles McIlroy, Brian Coll, Aidan McCallion, Donald McLennon.*
*Front row (left to right): Pat Owens, Eugene Nixon, Johnny Nugent.*
*At the present time Frankie McBride, John Taggart, Derek Mehaffey, Frank (Elvis) Chism), Richard Meyler and the star of the moment, Dominic Kirwin, keep the flagship of Omagh's musicians afloat nationwide with frequent tours all over the British Isles and further afield — possibly Russia next, who knows?*

*Winter sports — When the winter snows come the natural attraction for local children has always been Omagh Golf Course to sleigh. 1950 — Michael Lynch, Denis McCann, Austin Lynch, Ralph Rossi, Raymond McCann.*

*British Legion (Omagh Branch) photographed on the roadway opposite the Legion premises in Campsie Road in 1938. The men with the medals are all First World War veterans. The British Legion premises in Campsie were originally a corrugated iron shed at Daisy Hill, Clogher, before being erected on Clements' property, where they remain to the present day.*

*High Street, 1980, from an interesting viewpoint (scaffolding outside the Provincial Bank).*
*The Post Office is on the left (it is the only building in Omagh with the crest of King Edward VII). Rotarian Desmond Black's furniture store (previously the Home & Colonial Tea Stores) displays the first illuminated flashing display sign in Omagh. Beside Black's is Swan & Mitchell's shoe shop. The car at the kerb is an English registered razor-edge Triumph, while the car crossing the road is the old familiar Standard Vanguard. Note the volume of traffic, the absence of yellow lines and the numbers of bicycles along the kerb. Wordie's four-wheeled flat cart is making a delivery to Jim Mullan's shop — it delivered merchandise from the railway to all parts of the town. The Lilliput Laundry van is outside their premises beside McAdam & Bates chemist shop on the right.*

*Jack Devlin of Campsie was one of the main funeral furnishers in Omagh. This photograph shows his hearse JI 4473 and limousine in the grounds of Knocknamoe Castle in 1930. The driver of the hearse is Joe McCaffery, who worked with the Devlin family from he was sixteen years old. The other driver is a Mr. Healy.*

Drumragh Avenue was opened in 1966; if it hadn't been constucted Omagh would be one of the biggest bottlenecks in Ulster today with respect to traffic. In order to construct this through road, four well-known Omagh properties had to go.

Photograph one shows Anderson Brothers grocers, Mullan's off-licence and Adrain's drapers. Anderson's Austin delivery van is at the front door, while the car is a Vauxhall Velox.

This is a continuation of the above photograph showing Catherine Slevin's chemist shop (previously Herbie Kyle's) which was also demolished but later rebuilt on the corner where it is today.

*The Staff of Anderson Brothers in 1940.*
*From left to right: L. Porter, Cecil Stewart, A. McComisky, Isobel Anderson, Herbert Shortt, G. Clarke.*

*When the Xmas lights were switched on in John Street for the first time in 1948 these were the men who were responsible for the move away from the main street. From left: Arthur Kelly, John McGale, Joseph Cunningham, Rotarian Frank Mullan, Fred Todd.*

*Omagh Telephone Exchange, 1948.*

*How times have changed — do you remember the days when if you wanted to make a telephone call you lifted the receiver and waited for the voice to say "Number please"? You gave your number and you waited while the telephonist at the other end put you through. Now it's all digital and press-button and of course quicker. But have a look at those pretty faces behind those sweet voices which did the work for you in 1948. Seated at the table: Rita McLaughlin. Standing at the window: Isobel Pigott. Left to right (standing): Gertie Montgomery (deceased), Hilda Graham (deceased). Seated at switchboard (left to right): Joanna Boyle, Dorothy Martin, Maureen McDermott, Frances Monteith, Dorothy Roberts (deceased), Frances Scarffe, Dorcas Richardson.*

*Johnston Park Health Clinic, 28th June 1951.*
*A group of mothers and babies who attended the Welfare Foods meeting arranged by the Ministry of Food at the Child Welfare Clinic.*
*At the rear are Dr. F. McKeown, Deputy County M.O.H., and Mr. R. Rodgers, Chairman of Omagh Food Control Committee, outside*
*the Child Welfare Clinic. This building stood where Johnston Park Car Park is today. Note the row of garages on the right — they*
*belonged to the Royal Arms Hotel.*

# PRIMARY SOURCES FOR STUDY OF THE EARLY HISTORY OF CO. TYRONE AND ULSTER

Book of Rights (Leabhar na gCeart) c.468. Ascribed to St. Benignus, successor of St. Patrick. Edited by O'Donovan.

Book of Armagh 807. Feardomhnach. Manuscript in T.C.D.

Book of Leinster c.1150. Fragments from Leabhar Gabhals (Book of Invasions) and Genealogies.

Book of Ballymote c.1390. Fragments from Book of Invasions and Genealogies.

An Leabhar Gabhala (Book of Invasions). Describes the early colonies.

Annals of Ulster 431-1498 by Cathal Maguire. Afterwards brought down to 1541. Edited by W. M. Hennessy and B. McCarthy, 1887-1901.

Annals of the Four Masters 1170-1616. Written by Michael O'Clery, Conaire O'Clery, Peregrine O'Clery and Fearfeasa O'Mulconry, 1632-36. Edited and translated by Owen Connellan, 1846.

Annals of the Kingdom of Ireland. Early times to 1616. Written by the Four Masters. Ed. and tr. by John O'Donovan, M.R.I.A. Dublin, 1848-51.

Annals of Boyle. Early times to 1562. Edited by Charles O'Connor.

Annals of Clonmacnoise. Early times to 1403. Tr. in 1627 by Conell Mageoghegan. Ed. by D. Murphy in 1896.

Annals of Loch Ce 1014-1590. Tr. by W. M. Hennessy, M.R.I.A. London 1871.

Annals of Connaught to 1580. Ed. by A. M. Freeman. Dublin 1944.

Annals of Innisfallen 428-1321. Ed. by S. MacAirt. Dublin 1951.

Annals of the Friar Clyn to 1347. Ed. by R. Butler 1849.

Annals of Tighearnach, Abbot of Clonmacnoise, 1080-1178. Ed. by Whitely Stokes in Revue Celtique 1895-97.

Annals of Ware 1485-1558. By Sir James Ware, 1664. Original in Latin. Tr. in 1705.

Forus Feasa ar Eirinn. The first History of Ireland. Written by Geoffrey Keating. Tr. by Desmond O'Connor. Dublin 1841.

Acta Sanctorum. John Colgan 1645.

Onomasticon Goedelicum. Edmund Hogan, S.J. 1910, Dublin. Gaelic names of places and tribes.

Monasticon Hibernicum. By Mervyn Archdale. 1786, London. Ancient Irish monastic establishments.

Conquest of Ireland (Expugnatio Hibernica). By Gerald Barry (Giraldus Cambrensis). Vol. V of his collected works. Edited by Brewer — Rolls Series.

Ireland as described by Davies. By Sir John Davies. Ed. by Morley.

## SOME SECONDARY SOURCES FOR THE STUDY OF TYRONE AND ULSTER HISTORY

Phases of Irish History. By Eoin McNeill. Dublin, 1919.

Celtic Ireland. By Eoin McNeill. Dublin, 1921.

A History of Medieval Ireland 1086-1513. London, 1938. Edmund Curtis.

A History of Medieval Ireland 1169-1485. J. Otway-Ruthven. London, 1968.

Medieval Ireland c.1170-1495. P. W. A. Asplin. Dublin, 1971.

The Church in Early Irish Society. Kathleen Hughes. London, 1968.

Sources of Early Irish History — Ecclesiastical. James F. Kenny. New York, 1929.

Irish Monasticism. John Ryan. Dublin, 1931.

Medieval Religious Houses. Gwyn and Hadcock. London, 1970.

Gleanings from Ulster History. Seamus O'Ceallaigh. Cork, 1951.

Ireland under the Normans 1169-1333. C. H. Orpen. Oxford, 1911-20.

The Cycle of Kings. Myles Dillon. Oxford, 1946.

The Lordship of Ireland in the Middle Ages. J. F. Lydon. Dublin, 1972.

The Making of an O'Neill. Ulster Journal of Archeology 1970.

The rise of the Ui Neill and the High-Kingship of Ireland. F. J. Byrne. Dublin, 1969.

# Acknowledgements

Many thanks to all the people at home and abroad who wrote to me and helped in the preparation of this book; it would be impossible to name them all, but it's nice to know that a part of them is here in Old Ireland in Omagh, the town of their birth or adoption. The names listed below supplied postcards and photographs for this book and to them I am most grateful.

May Adams
Bertie Anderson
Isobel Anderson
Norman Anderson
Belfast News Letter
Desmond Black
Dorothy Bradley
Marie Brogan
Eliz. Burton
Richard Butler
Myra Bonar
Douglas Bell
Maurice Bloomfield
Ruby Campbell
Tom Crawford
Ronald Colhoun (deceased)
Bernard Cox
Norman Campbell
Christian Brothers School
Veda Colhoun (deceased)
Cappagh Parish Magazine
Leo Doran
Drumragh Parish Magazine
Norah Donaldson
Gerald and Sue Darling
Marie Devlin

John Donnellan
William Davidson
Robert Duncan
Iris Ellis
Jean Faux
William Fyffe
Donal Gillespie
Rosemary Graham
Alan Hannigan
Una Hunt
John Hunter
Gertrude Hamilton
Stanley Hannan
Robert Jamison
Loto Johnston (deceased)
Rita Johnston
Betty Johnston
Tom Kernan
Alice Keenan
Edna Love
Loreto Convent
Harold Monteith
Nicholas Murray
Albert Martin
Alan Neil
Paddy Moore

Peter McAleer
Patsy McGarrity
Ian and Lorraine McFarland
Mark McGrath, Jun.
Joan and Kay McCauley
Harold and Gertie McCauley
Rosalie McClintock
Michael McSorley
Rodney McElrea
Ronnie McCartney
William McGrew
Mollie McKimmon
Omagh Academicals R.F.C.
Omagh District Council
Omagh Motor Club
Marie O'Neill
Roderick O'Connor
Robert Parke
Alan Porter (Holland Collection)
Marcus Pigott
Arthur O. Quinn
Nora Quigley
Geraldine Quinn
Ralph Rossi
Richard Scott
Edward Scott

Alan Shannon
Elsie Stewart
Robinson Stewart
Catherine Sloane (deceased)
Geoffrey Simpson
Thomas Strain
Ernest Somerville (deceased)
Robert and Betty Smith
St. Enda's G.A.A.
Jack and Liam Torney
Tyrone Constitution
 (Norman Armstrong)
The Academy, Omagh
Ulster Herald
 (Austin Lynch)
Ulster Folk and Transport
 Museum, Cultra (John Moore)
Dai Waterson
Ina White
Stanley White
Valerie White
Tom Wilmot
Emma Wilson
Fred Wright
Richard Wilton
Jim Walsh
West Tyrone Historical Society